"Austin has earned a reputation as a launchpad for brilliant ideas and a magnet for big thinkers. Shravan Parsi is part of this culture of progress. Since beginning his investment career in Texas, Shravan continues to pave the way for business innovation and growth here in the capital city. We all benefit from his ideas about business, development, and the potential of individuals to make an impact ... in Austin and beyond."

STEVE ADLER, mayor of Austin

"*The Science of the Deal* provides the reader with a powerful guide packed full of technical information, case studies, and stories that will empower the reader to understand what makes a good deal and when to walk away. From his roots in Hyderabad, India, to being the CEO of the successful multifamily and commercial real estate investment firm American Ventures, the wisdom Shravan shares will benefit any entrepreneur."

DAVID OSBORN,
New York Times best-selling author of *Wealth Can't Wait*

"Here is a step-by-step insider's look into multifamily housing investing. Using Shravan's five characteristics of success, the reader has a path to follow."

PAT NIEKAMP, founder, *Texas CEO Magazine*

"A scientific, yet self-reflective, guide that lays out the basics for commercial real estate investing. Shravan takes readers on an entrepreneur's journey that shows how to become a successful real estate investor. His story is a great read that reminds us that even real estate can be broken down to a science, revealing the DNA that distinguishes a good versus a bad potential investment."

SONDRA WENGER, managing director of a private equity, real estate, and infrastructure firm

---

"If there is one book I would have a real estate entrepreneur read before starting a multifamily investment firm, this would be it. Frankly, this book provides anyone investing in multifamily housing the roadmap for determining which manager to invest with."

MICHAEL SONNENFELDT, founder, TIGER 21

"I met Shravan early in his multifamily investing career and saw that he was equipped with a unique stack of skills and mental models different from others in CRE. I have watched the combination of Shravan's work ethic, analysis of deals, and long-term mindset lead to out-sized success now, and I believe he is just getting started."

RICHARD C. WILSON, CEO, Family Office Club

THE **SCIENCE** OF THE **DEAL**

THE **SCIENCE** OF THE **DEAL**

THE DNA OF MULTIFAMILY & COMMERCIAL REAL ESTATE INVESTING

SHRAVAN PARSI

ForbesBooks

Published by ForbesBooks, Charleston, South Carolina.
Member of Advantage Media Group.

ForbesBooks is a registered trademark, and the ForbesBooks colophon is a trademark of Forbes Media, LLC.

Printed in the United States of America.

10 9 8 7 6 5 4 3 2 1

ISBN: 978-1-94663-378-1
LCCN: 2019914989

Book design by Carly Blake.

This publication is designed to provide accurate and authoritative information in regard to the subject matter covered. It is sold with the understanding that the publisher is not engaged in rendering legal, accounting, or other professional services. If legal advice or other expert assistance is required, the services of a competent professional person should be sought.

Advantage Media Group is proud to be a part of the Tree Neutral® program. Tree Neutral offsets the number of trees consumed in the production and printing of this book by taking proactive steps such as planting trees in direct proportion to the number of trees used to print books. To learn more about Tree Neutral, please visit **www.treeneutral.com**.

Since 1917, the Forbes mission has remained constant. Global Champions of Entrepreneurial Capitalism. ForbesBooks exists to further that aim by bringing the Stories, Passion, and Knowledge of top thought leaders to the forefront. ForbesBooks brings you The Best in Business. To be considered for publication, please visit **www.forbesbooks.com**.

To my dad, the late Dr. Sudershan Parsi, and my mom,
Sujatha Parsi, for giving me and my siblings the power of
education and the flexibility to pursue our careers and our dreams.
Thank you for instilling the doctrine, "Never settle for less in life,
and fight against all odds to achieve what you desire."

CONTENTS

FOREWORD xi

A WORD FROM THE AUTHOR xv

CHAPTER 1 1
From Side Hustle to the Main Show

CHAPTER 2 15
Know Your Industry

CHAPTER 3 53
Team and Talent

CHAPTER 4 77
Using Time and Leverage to Seize Opportunity

CHAPTER 5 101
The Potential of Downsides

CHAPTER 6 121
Ask Really Good Questions and Delegate to Experts

CHAPTER 7 . . . . **131**
Networking and Giving Back:
Creating a Center of Influence

CHAPTER 8 . . . . **153**
Up and Out: Stretching Limits

ACKNOWLEDGMENTS **177**

ABOUT THE AUTHOR **179**

OUR SERVICES **181**

FOREWORD

initially met Shravan while serving on the board of the Austin Technology Council. Our first meeting sans boardroom occurred when Shravan proactively invited me to the aptly named Hideout Coffee House. Little did I know the innocuous meeting invite was for my benefit. Shravan had done his homework and discovered the company I founded had just opened a brand-new office 9,130 miles from Austin, coincidentally in his hometown of Hyderabad, India.

It was then, while talking one-on-one with Shravan over iced lattes, that I finally unraveled his intention with the meeting. He wanted to see how he could help me! That was it and it alone. Here, on a hot July day, you had two busy founder CEOs who already were volunteering their time to help promote the technological interests of central Texas. Then Shravan went a full leap further by seeing how he could help a fellow director ensure his new office half a world away would be successful. It was a completely altruistic act of the kind that I've witnessed him perform countless times since. It's this idiosyncrasy that, in my opinion, forms the strong bedrock of Shravan's relationships and is something we all should aspire to practice more frequently (myself included). To put it simply: in every new encounter Shravan endeavors to discover ways he can help the person he's interacting with, even if he or she is reluctant to ask for help. It's a remarkably refreshing way to approach an interaction and runs contradictory to 98 percent of the meetings I take, where people are generally overtly (or worse, covertly) asking for something.

Once Shravan was confident that I wasn't completely fish-out-of-water in his hometown, the conversation evolved to the remarkable similarities between Austin and Hyderabad. You would struggle to find two places any farther apart geographically, yet something about the energy and philosophy of the capital of Texas and those of the capital of Andhra Pradesh have uncanny resemblances. We briefly toyed with the idea of making the two capitals sister cities, and eventually realized our focus could be applied to more pressing matters. Following our first coffee meeting, we became fast friends. Despite operating in quite different industries, we share many common interests relating to investing, entrepreneurship, aerospace, and biotechnology. From the outset Shravan was extraordinarily inclusive and went out of his way to extend an invitation to me whenever he felt I might find an event interesting or useful. Over time the breadth and depth of our shared experiences turned into shared adventures. On numerous occasions I have had the opportunity to meet his wonderful mother at gala charity functions, where she deliberately makes an effort to show her gratitude to Shravan's guests for being in attendance.

One of my favorite of Shravan's traits is his willingness to go along with his friends' activities even when they're not fully fleshed out. For example, he was the first person to say "yes" when I invited a pilgrimage of twenty entrepreneurs across the US to meet up in the remote desert oasis of Marfa for twenty-four hours. On that same trip he jumped at the chance to fly in an airplane with me as I flew one thousand feet over Jeff Bezos's nearby secret (at the time) Blue Origin launch facility. We were later chased away by black SUVs with men sitting on top carrying what appeared to be automatic weapons.

Similarly, at a moment's notice Shravan said "yes" to joining me and a small group to witness the first launch of the Falcon Heavy Rocket. Without a second thought he agreed to split the cost of the roundtrip flight in a private Lear 60, even though the launch time itself was a roll of the dice. His trust and intuition paid off, as we got to see the history-making flight later that day.

Shravan Parsi is a man who embodies the rare intersection of authenticity, altruism, and intelligence. He instinctively tries to help people in his network realize their full potential, and builds lifelong friends as a result. This book is an extension of Shravan's genuine desire to freely share his hard-sought knowledge and allow others to build their own analogous successes. It's a bona fide "how-to guide" that will enable readers to repurpose Shravan's wisdom for their own pursuits in real estate investing or other endeavors.

JOHN ARROW
Founder and chairman, Mutual Mobile
Named on the *Forbes* "Most Promising CEOs Under 35" list

A WORD FROM THE AUTHOR

moved to the United States from Hyderabad, India, to pursue training and a career in pharmaceutical science. Like many of my peers, I invested in real estate in my spare time. I took an innovative approach to fixing and flipping homes by helping families with poor credit realize the American Dream of owning a home. Eventually, my success in real estate made it too expensive to keep my job as a pharmaceutical scientist. Yearning for something bigger than small-scale residential real estate deals, I founded a commercial real estate firm specializing in multifamily workforce housing. In time, I scaled up and founded American Ventures LLC.

This book tells the story of how I took an entrepreneurial and systematic approach to investing in commercial real estate (CRE) and multifamily housing. I believe the key to success in any CRE investment firm—really, any business—is being systematic. I learned this approach from my training and work in pharmaceutical science. In pivoting from the pharmaceutical industry to the CRE investment industry, I learned that it is easy enough to apply the insights from science to any field.

Any entrepreneurial venture benefits from using key performance indicators (KPIs) to make critical business decisions. In a CRE firm, you use KPIs to evaluate the financial aspects of an investment deal and create underwriting models that form the backbone of a deal. A critical aspect of developing a good underwriting model is using empirical methods to measure KPIs and analysis to support decisions and manage risk. In chapter 2, I outline building underwriting models with KPIs and develop cases to illustrate how to use them. The chapter includes detailed spreadsheets that I think any firm should use to guide business decisions. You can download those spreadsheets from the book's website.

Creating successful CRE investment deals goes beyond quantitative KPIs. You must also engage in rigorous due diligence to analyze the qualitative aspects of deals. Throughout chapters 2, 4, and 5, I discuss the fundamentals of what to look for in a city or neighborhood and how to systematically evaluate them.

You can't talk about CRE investment without considering risk. To be successful you must distinguish predictable from unpredictable risks. In a systematic approach, you assess and account for predictable risks. You build flexibility into your models and planning to mitigate unpredictable risks. I introduce these issues in chapter 2 and continue discussing them in chapters 4 and 5.

These empirical factors are one aspect of creating successful CRE deals. Other factors include understanding the different roles involved in a multifamily CRE investment firm, hiring for excellence, and developing teamwork. You'll find my thoughts on hiring and supporting the right people in chapter 3. Without a solid team, you're unlikely to accomplish your goals.

In addition to building a solid team, you need to build important qualities in yourself. Developing and practicing curiosity, accelerated learning, grit, discipline, and openness to feedback are just the beginning. Developing these qualities is the focus of chapter 6.

You're also unlikely to reach your goals and appreciate your accomplishments if you focus only on yourself. In fact, your life is less about yourself than it is about the people around you. You will get the most satisfaction out of your work and life if you can do good while creating wealth and apply the wealth you create to doing good. I focus on these topics and more in chapter 7.

In closing the book, I consider the future. What impact is technology having on the CRE industry? What are my plans for American Ventures, my multifamily and commercial real estate investment firm, and how will I accomplish them? What opportunities are developing as globalization continues to open economic activity? Where will changing demographics lead multifamily housing? And as we look into the middle-distance future, where will space exploration lead the CRE industry?

An enduring presence in my life is my father, who died in 2016. One of the more important values he taught me is to make good use of my time. You'll encounter this idea along with other elements of his wisdom throughout the book. I hope the book inspires you to take his advice to make good use of your time.

CHAPTER 1

FROM SIDE HUSTLE TO THE MAIN SHOW

had already decided. I stood looking out the window at the city, saying farewell. You know the scene; you've seen it in movies: the skyscrapers and brownstones, the neatly laid out grid of streets and green spaces. Maybe I loved it so much because it was so different from where I grew up in a town in India, yet so like Hyderabad, where I lived as a teenager. Or maybe what I loved most was the people from dozens of countries—places like Japan, China, Russia, Germany, France, England, the Dominican Republic, Spain, South Africa, Nigeria, Brazil, Nepal, Indonesia, and, yes, India—mingling on the streets, like the complex aroma of my mother's biryani—garlic and chili, cardamom and cumin, cinnamon. There were smells from all around the world, too: sauerkraut from the Jewish deli nearly overwhelming the peppery scent of kimchi from the Korean barbeque restaurant next door; the delicate aroma of Chinese happy family blending with *herbes de Provence*, and, of course, Indian curry with

1

its pungent, slightly bitter smell of turmeric.

I had a successful career as a pharmaceutical scientist; that's what drew me to New York, to study at St. John's University. Success in a good job, living in a city I loved—so why was I moving to Texas? How did I become the founder and CEO of a successful US commercial real estate company?

I'll break it down into five steps.

Step 1: Be Bold and Flexible

My family loves to tell the story of how, when I was a toddler, I chose to attend a traditional Indian school. India has preprimary schools in addition to primary and secondary education. Most parents send their children to preprimary schools that are like private schools or charter schools. India has many languages, with Hindi being the national language. Most of the states have their own language (not a dialect), so growing up, I learned three languages. Telugu is my native language, my mother tongue. Hindi is my second language, and English is my third. Most students enroll in English school, which teaches all subjects in English. In the mornings, my parents would drop me off with my siblings at the English-medium school. However, once the school day started, I would run across the shared campus to Shishu Mandir, a traditional Indian school, with roots going back to the ancient Indian school system. Eventually, the principal of the English school called my father and told him the situation. Once I became more aware, I chose to stay at the traditional school. Fortunately, my parents were flexible and maybe saw a hidden wisdom in me and supported it. It probably helped that the traditional school was very good. The early lesson in flexibility manifested later in my life.

At the Shishu Mandir school, the day began with a general assembly in the center of the school. We started our day with a prayer and performing Surya Namaskar, or Sun Salutations. Part of the curriculum during that period was history, theology, and how India won its independence from Great Britain in 1947. The curriculum gave tremendous importance to science, mathematics, and social studies. Even as a kid, I realized those basics helped us many times over as we advanced into higher studies. At the end of the school day, we again assembled and chanted Shanti Mantra, a prayer for world peace.[1]

All the classes at this traditional school were taught in Telugu; the school also taught Hindi. In addition to a strong emphasis on STEM courses, one course in the curriculum imparted a lot of information on the powerful leaders who shaped India, much like the American history curriculum features George Washington, Thomas Jefferson, Abraham Lincoln, and others. Two of India's greatest leaders are Mahatma Gandhi, who is known and admired throughout the world, and Sardar (a title that means chief or headman) Vallabhbhai Patel. Patel's home state in India recently dedicated a six-hundred-foot-tall statue honoring him; it is the tallest statue in the world, even taller than the Statue of Liberty. Patel is noted for leading the factions in India to form a unified nation and working with Gandhi to promote a nonviolent approach to independence. It is the same nonviolent approach that inspired Reverend Martin Luther King Jr. in his civil rights movement in America.

I was deeply inspired by Gandhi's teachings and life. Gandhi

---

1   Peace researcher, political scientist, and philosopher Samrat Schmiem Kumar explains that "The peace mantra Om shanti- shanti- shanti is traditionally repeated three times. One may also interpret this as the meaning of peace in the body, mind, and soul (i.e. one's entire being), or as a wish for peace individually, collectively, and universally."

Samrat Schmiem Kumar, *Bhakti – The Yoga of Love: Trans-rational Approaches to Peace Studies*, (Berlin, Germany: Lit Verlag, 2010), 78.

once said that English was the language of business and diplomacy throughout the world. If you wanted to become a global leader, you needed to learn English. In seventh grade, I decided that I wanted to be a global leader and transferred to an English school to learn the language. I wanted to have the capacity to do more. At the time—the early 1990s—my family lived in a town but had a plan to move to Hyderabad. It's the sixth largest city in India and the city where my dad went to medical school. Because my parents expected that I would attend medical school, they supported my decision to enroll in an English school even though they knew it would be challenging—like moving from Earth to Mars. When they said I could try, however, I said that try implies you can choose to fail. I didn't plan to fail.

My dad is one of my biggest role models. As a young child, he had a mild case of polio. Yet he fought all the odds to become the first medical doctor in his small town. He had to go through a lot of extra tests to ensure that his mild disability would not have an impact on patients. If he could fight those odds and succeed—he eventually became the civil surgeon and resident medical officer of one of Hyderabad's largest hospitals—then I could learn English and do well in school.

Switching to a school with English as the main language was a massive transition. Every teacher, however, was aware that I had done well at the traditional school and gave me additional support. All the students welcomed me. With extra care from teachers and support from fellow students, by tenth grade I received the highest ranking on district tests. When my family moved to Hyderabad, I was ready.

Step 2: Be Interested in Everything and Observe Closely

My mom and dad achieved some phenomenal things in their lives that left an impact on me. My mom had an option to enroll in medical school and become a doctor, just like my dad. She instead chose to raise me and my three siblings and became a full-time mother. In addition to being a great mom, she participated in social and philanthropic activities and won regional recognition for a club she is president of. My dad worked hard, and his medical practice enabled him to build a good income. With that income, he bought plots of land in and around Hyderabad. When he retired, his real estate portfolio was much larger than his savings, and some of the property values were larger by multiples than what he earned from his medical practice. These facts stayed in the back of my mind for many years.

When I was around fourteen, my father built a two-story home with downstairs portions for rental and the entire upstairs for us to live. He pointed out that I had time to kill over summer vacation and recommended that I watch the process. So my brother

MANY YEARS LATER, THIS IDEA BECAME THE BUILDING BLOCK OF ALL MY SINGLE-FAMILY INVESTING IN THE UNITED STATES.

and I watched the construction and supervised the contractors. It left a strong impression on me. I saw how tough the development process is and how easy it is to miss simple things. Moreover, I saw how to create value in a deal and how to generate residual income by renting out three-quarters of a house, which paid the expenses of the portion we lived in. Many years later, this idea became the building block of all my single-family investing in the United States.

Step 3: Pivot When Necessary and Make Good Use of Your Time

It is traditional in middle-class Indian culture to choose a professional career and even more traditional to follow in your father's footsteps. Naturally, I wanted to be a medical doctor like my father. In India you go to junior college for two years, and then you specialize. Medical school is very competitive—back then, 50,000 people might apply for 500 seats—and it is very expensive to think of enrolling in medical school if you are not among those 500. I missed the cutoff criterion on the entrance exam by 0.1.

Even though I lost out on enrolling in medical school that year by one-tenth of a point, I had an option to retake the exam the next year. Most students spend another year preparing to retake the exam; a vast number of students who missed out by such a small amount enroll in medical school the following year. Nothing is guaranteed, however, especially on a 1:100 ratio. In the meantime, I received an offer to join the undergraduate program in pharmacy at one of the most prestigious schools in India.

At this point, I pivoted. First, I decided to become a pharmaceutical scientist and got my bachelor's degree in pharmacy. Second, I set my goal as owning a pharmaceutical company; even at that time, I leaned more to the business side of work. Massive pharmaceutical companies like Pfizer and GlaxoSmithKline inspired me. Also, I thought, *Doctors prescribe the drugs, but scientists* create *the drugs*. Third, I enrolled in a school in India, the Manipal Academy of Higher Education, that is more like an international town. Twenty to 30 percent of the students were from the United States, Canada, the United Kingdom, Australia, Malaysia, or Singapore; many of the overseas students were the children of Indians who had emigrated to those countries. They enrolled in medical, dental, pharmacy, physiotherapy, and other health sciences programs. Being exposed to people from all these different countries left me wanting to explore the world. But the students from the United States had the biggest impact. They left me with a desire to be in New York City.

When I looked at graduate schools, only one university in New York offered what I wanted—St. John's University—and I applied only to that one school. I was lucky with my undergraduate and graduate choices; both times the one school I applied to admitted me. In hindsight, I would never recommend anyone apply to one school in the hope of getting in. Always apply to several schools, and enroll in your first choice. But give yourself options if you don't get into that school.

When I graduated with my bachelor's degree, it was too late to enter graduate school for fall. Although I received admission for the spring semester, if I waited until the next fall, I would have a full tuition waiver and teaching assistantship. St. John's is a private school; going early and paying full tuition for a semester did not seem like a viable option. I had a gap, time on my hands, and no plans.

My father had some fundamental principles. One of them is that you cannot waste time. He believed that if I did not have a task to work on, I would become a completely different person. Without a task, I might spend all my time playing games or doing other things that are not worthwhile. As a result, he paid out of pocket for that first semester—about $7,500 in the United States back then and over 300,000 rupees, India's currency.

I still had a gap, but it was down to about five months. Again, my father said that I should not spend five months at home doing nothing. So I did a little pivot. I enrolled in an MBA program at a top-notch business school in Pune, a city not too far from Mumbai, the financial hub of India. But I didn't let anyone know that I would be going to graduate school in New York in five months. Even so, I gave all I had for that one semester. While I was there, a group of students and I made a presentation to Tata, an Indian conglomerate that owns the Range Rover and Jaguar brands, as well as information technology consulting businesses. I was also the team leader for the Cultural Committee. Our task was to host the school's first big cultural show. My role as team leader involved uniting one hundred MBA students from different parts of India on short notice to create and perform a show in front of well-known local and national business leaders. Leading one hundred or so type A personalities in the most competitive Indian educational program was no small task. We got into constructive brainstorming, arguments, and some fights, and at the end of it all, the show was a massive success.

We also went over budget.

When our professors congratulated our committee after the event, they asked me to speak in front of all the students. I gave credit for the success to all the team members but took the blame for going over budget. That I held myself accountable led the head of school to approve the budget in seconds. The business knowledge I gained had a much bigger impact on my future success than you would think a semester could have. It is almost impossible to tell at the time what impact something will have on you later in life.

WHETHER IT'S A SMALL OR A BIG JOB, ALWAYS MAKE YOUR IMPACT. THE REASON? WE ARE WORKING ON OURSELVES WHILE WE DO THE TASK AT HAND.

In graduate school while doing my master's in industrial pharmacy at St. John's, my dad's advice to make good use of my time still drove me. I went to school in the evening and worked for a cell phone store during the day in

Manhattan. I made so many cell phone sales and did so many activations that I set the sales record for that store. Whether it's a small or a big job, always make your impact. The reason? We are working on ourselves while we do the task at hand. One lesson I learned from all these experiences is that these small steps play a pivotal role once you determine what you want to do in life. Be the best at every task you take on.

After two summer semesters in addition to the regular school season, I graduated in one year and four months, a record time for anyone to graduate with a master's degree at St. John's. My first job as a pharmaceutical scientist was a contract job at Schering-Plough's New Jersey site. Schering-Plough was one of the top ten pharmaceutical companies in the United States back then but has since merged with Merck. I had the privilege of playing a small role in developing their antihistamine drug Clarinex.

On September 11, 2001, I was commuting to the company's offices in Kenilworth, New Jersey, when I heard news reports about a fire in the city: a plane had hit one of the World Trade Center towers. Having grown up in India, with an inherent interest in geopolitics of the region and the world, I used to read about terrorist activities in the northern Indian state Jammu and Kashmir, mainly abetted by cross-border elements supported by neighboring countries. With that in mind, I immediately thought about terrorism. By the time I arrived at work, the World Trade Center buildings were down, and, from the terrace, I could see the massive plumes of smoke.

With so much web traffic in those dial-up internet days, most of the domestic mainstream news sites were down. I had to use news sites from India to learn what was happening since there were no televisions in our lab. We had a full workday without knowing what was happening across the Hudson River. In the midst of those horrific events, one thing I learned was how resilient a country like America is. While the entire world was watching, we had our full workday.

Just twenty days prior to the 9/11 terrorist attacks, I had been at the Windows on the World's bar, the Greatest Bar on Earth, on the 107th floor of the World Trade Center, having drinks with friends from work to celebrate a new job I was taking. A week after the attacks, I made the rounds of my favorite places and restaurants in that area to say farewell to my favorite city. I was moving to Texas. It was a sad time to leave New York.

Step 4: Learn How to Sell Anything

I moved to San Antonio, Texas, to take a position with more responsibility, bigger projects, and better pay at a midsize pharmaceutical company. It was a better schedule as well, eight to five with the evenings free. And in San Antonio at that time, my commute was short: no subways, just a quick drive to my home. Like they say, everything is big in Texas, so I lived in an apartment complex on the top of a hill. I enjoyed the freedom of not having to share my place with roommates. I started exploring my hobbies. In spite of this, I was not happy. I wanted to do more in my life.

With evenings free in San Antonio, I made friends. I also wasted a lot of time. Then I started thinking, *You know what? I want to do something else. I'm wasting my time.* When you're doing nothing and out with friends, opportunities can suddenly appear. I was recruited to be a part of a network marketing company. This was my first "sales job" since working at a cell phone store in Manhattan. I sold Amway for a month. At network marketing companies, you act as an independent contractor running your small business and recruiting others to work under you. If you get lucky and the person you hire is a hustler, you can benefit. Because the company leaves so much to luck, it is more like they are selling a dream than a genuine business model. Within a month, I realized it wasn't working for me and lost focus.

I looked into another network marketing company called USANA Health Sciences, which sells nutritional supplements, or "nutraceuticals." Their science and supplements were good, and I believed that prevention is better than cure; I still do. A good lifestyle can prevent many of the diseases we have like heart disease, diabetes, and stroke. USANA's marketing pitch was health and financial freedom; you achieve health with a good lifestyle and good supplements and earn "financial freedom" by being their sales rep.

Although I wanted to be good enough to achieve economies of scale—I recruited about thirty people in about three months and was one of the top recruiters for a week in the entire United States for the company—I was not sold on the network marketing concept. The people at the top of my "upline" did not inspire me. They were selling a story, which is hard to replicate, and did not seem like the kind of role models who would help me achieve my goals. I decided to quickly get out.

One thing that came out of the experience, though, was the knowledge that if I can sell the products *and* a story and recruit others, then I can sell anything. Selling is a pivotal skill most entrepreneurs must have.

Step 5: Always Ask What's Next and Do It with Hustle

Simultaneous with getting out of network marketing, I was thinking, *What else?* Nothing else was not an option; I remembered my father's words: "Make good use of your time." I also remembered my father's real estate investing success. I remembered how much I enjoyed watching the house being built and how much I learned from the details. I started looking into real estate and then began connecting the dots.

Being in Texas when I explored real estate was an advantage. The cost of entry in a city like San Antonio was relatively low. At the time, the median home price was about $150,000. In New York, the cost of entry was much higher. During my days living close to the St. John's campus, I observed that people's homes had a basement with a separate entrance, and the owners rented them to four students at a time. I paid top dollar to share a basement apartment with three other students. Housing prices and rents in New York were crazy. I may not have tried real estate if I had stayed in New York.

Like my experience working in a cell phone store while in school, real estate was not my main activity. I was a full-time scientist working from eight to five. I invested in real estate in the evenings, looking for homes, connecting with brokers, sellers, contractors, and buyers. And then I noticed it was costing me to go to work from eight to five. For example, if I bought a home, fixed it up, and put it on the market, I was not available to talk with people about it or show it during the day.

However, I did not quit my job right away. I had an objective: stay in my pharmaceutical job until the real estate income was twice the value of my salary. When I hit that objective—when real estate was no longer a side hustle—I decided it made sense to invest more time in real estate than the scientific position.

When I arrived in San Antonio, Texas, it was the most exotic place I had ever been. The city is spread out; about 1.5 million people live on 465 square miles of land. In a way, New York City was more like my home in Hyderabad, India. In New York, a little over 8.5 million people are squeezed into a little over 300 square miles; Hyderabad has about 7 million people living in 251 square miles. San Antonio felt like a small town compared to both, and the amount of living space was luxurious. But in all three cities—four including Austin, my home for the last few years—success in commercial real estate takes hustle. In the remainder of the book, I will show you how.

CHAPTER 2

KNOW YOUR INDUSTRY

T
he first building in Duncanville, Texas, was Nance Brothers General Store, built in a field called Duncan Switch, a stop on the Chicago, Texas, and Mexican Railroad. In 1904, almost twenty-five years after its founding, Duncanville's population was 113. By that time, nearby Dallas had a population of more than 42,000. In 1973, when Dallas had grown so massive that an advertising firm coined the term *metroplex* to describe it, Duncanville was home to just 15,000 people. But by the 2010 census, Duncanville's population, at 38,524, had more than doubled. And in 2018, *Thrillist* called it one of Dallas's best suburbs for millennials who appreciated diversity and natural landscapes. Duncanville was now part of the metroplex.

The Dallas–Fort Worth–Arlington metroplex is the largest metropolitan area in Texas and the fourth largest in the United States. It is home to nearly 6,500,000 people. Six of its smaller cities—including Duncanville—form the Best Southwest area in Dallas County. The economic and population growth in the Dallas–Fort Worth–Arlington metropolitan area is what makes it so attractive for multifamily commercial real estate investing.

Today, Duncanville's 11.3 square miles contain more than fifteen public parks, nine elementary schools, and a little over five thousand apartments. These characteristics drew our firm's attention to an investment opportunity at Duncanville Commons, a three-hundred-unit garden apartment complex near the crossroads of Interstate 20 and Route 67, just a quick drive up the highway to Dallas. The apartment complex has three-story brick buildings surrounding a three-level, resort-style swimming pool and courtyard. It looks like a very nice place to live. Today the apartments have all the modern amenities: gourmet kitchens with granite counters, laminate flooring, walk-in closets, and private patios and balconies. It makes a good case study to illustrate how we put together a value-add multifamily real estate deal.

Traditional Single-Family Real Estate as a Stepping-Stone and Way of Learning the Field

The housing industry is a global economic growth engine and is critical to the US economy's health. Housing is part of the finance, insurance, and real estate economic sector, which accounts for about 20 percent of GDP—that's $3.9 trillion. The housing industry drives economic activity in many other industries, including banking, construction, durable goods, legal services, interior design services, and now even media with HGTV shows like *Property Brothers* (2011), *Flip or Flop* (2013), and *Fixer Upper* (2013). (Incidentally, none of these television shows existed when I began investing in residential real estate.)

The breadth of opportunities in real estate drew me to the field when I was thinking about how to make good use of my free time. And my eventual focus on multifamily housing was not an accident. Many people enter the real estate investment industry by doing single-family home investment deals in their free time as a side business. They have a stable job and position in a company, and they want to buy a single-family home to generate rental income. Like a lot of my friends who work in the medical or pharmaceutical field, technology, or education, I did the same. These are great foundational steps for learning about real estate investment. I used to buy and renovate single-family homes, then sell or rent them. But unlike my friends, I was doing so much real estate that I gave up my full-time job. As I mentioned in the last chapter, it was costing me to work at my job as a scientist. Like entrepreneurs tend to do, I put all my effort into the venture.

At first, I focused on learning the industry. I bought, fixed, and sold or rented out homes in San Antonio, Texas, but I noticed that I had to keep five or six homes on the market for months before one sold. Every day that a home is ready but vacant is a loss. I needed to find a way to sell each home the moment it was ready. I also wanted to know how I could buy, renovate, and sell many properties at this faster pace.

My training in science made a difference at this point because it enabled me to analyze the situation. Suppose you bought ten homes, renovated them, and now are ready to sell. Although some of them sell in the first month, most of them take as long as six or seven months.

Let's restate the problem: What unique factors exist when someone buys a home? You have a buyer, a seller, a lender who lends the money that makes up the bulk of the capital stack, a lending process, and credit. As an investor, my credit was excellent, and I bought the homes with zero or very little money down; this is a predominant model in single-family home real estate investing. Potential buyers, however, must have good credit and put at least 5 percent of their own money into the deal for the lender to lend the money so the seller can sell the home. This analysis led me to focus on the credit part of the deal, and I spotted an opportunity to innovate.

To shorten the time it took to sell a house, I found people who had decent incomes and jobs—they could afford to buy or rent a home—and the money to invest, but insufficient credit scores. Perhaps their credit scores were low because of something they did when they were young. Even though it might be ten years later, the credit issue had a negative impact on their ability to qualify for a mortgage. To qualify for a mortgage, you need a credit score of at least 580. These potential buyers' credit scores were in the 540s and 550s, so they could not qualify for a loan.

THIS WAS MY OPPORTUNITY: THEY NEEDED SOMETHING I HAD, AND I HAD AN IDEA OF HOW TO PUT TOGETHER THE DEAL.

This was my opportunity: they needed something I had, and I had an idea of how to put together the deal. I asked potential buyers to put 5 to 10 percent of the purchase price into the deal—remember, the industry standard for investors at that time was closer to zero down. In return, they could live in my home, pay rent that covered the mortgage, and work with a professional, whom I paid, to repair their credit. My company vetted the credit repair professionals whom I matched potential buyers with. To mitigate the risk I took on, my credit repair professionals would assess the potential buyers' issues and make sure it would take only three to six months to repair their credit. Meanwhile, in addition to the 5 to 10 percent of the purchase price, I had rental income.

Because they put 5 to 10 percent of the purchase price into the deal, they had skin in the game—enough investment in the home that I knew they would not damage it. "For all practical purposes," I told them, "this is your home. Unless you miss a rent payment or damage the property, you're the owner, just not on paper." I held the 5 to 10 percent as a deposit and gave it back to them when they got their mortgage; they needed 3 to 5 percent for a down payment and 3 to 5 percent for closing costs. Within three to eighteen months, they got their mortgage, and ownership changed hands. Instead of making these deals on one or two homes, I made them on many homes. My income was in the six figures.

As an investment, single-family homes have several drawbacks: there is little access to capital, you buy and sell one at a time, and the industry is tightly regulated. In addition, even though a single-family rental supports itself and has cash flow, it is very difficult to create economies of scale. And I wanted to build a business at a much bigger scale than one home at a time or even six at a time.

Answering the question of how to buy, renovate, and sell many properties at a fast pace eventually took me into commercial real estate and land investments—I bought some prime real estate in metropolitan expansion and regentrifying areas. My science background came in handy again. It led me to observe, evaluate the situation, analyze the trends, direct my attention to a solution, and establish metrics. Even though I moved beyond single-family homes, I still wasn't getting the kind of investment I was looking for: a scaled-up property that has cash flow and supports itself.

Two Types of Research: Deciding Which Part of an Industry to Work in and Deciding Where to Invest

Most people think of properties where people live as residential real estate and properties where people do business as commercial real estate. However, some places, depending on how people use them, might seem to fall into a gray area. If a lawyer has an office in her home, does her home become a commercial property? The answer is "no," because she earns income from her law practice, not her property or the building on it. People live in apartment complexes; their apartments are their residences. Why are apartment complexes commercial real estate rather than residential real estate? The answer is that someone owns the property and buildings, and uses them to earn a profit; the profit can be in the form of income from rent or funds from capital gains.

Commercial real estate includes office, retail, and industrial properties, hotels, special-purpose properties like amusement parks, and multifamily housing. All these amazing varieties of properties have one thing in common: someone owns, or a group of people owns, the land and buildings to make a profit.

The number of units in a property determines whether it is multifamily housing. A property must include more than five units to be categorized as multifamily housing: high-rises with nine or more floors and an elevator (or more than one); midrises with fewer than nine floors and an elevator; garden-style apartments in a complex of one-, two-, or three-story buildings; and walk-ups with four to six stories and no elevator. Multifamily housing also includes manufactured housing communities (called trailer parks in some parts of the country) and special-purpose housing like student, senior, and subsidized housing. In my business, I focus on apartment complexes with one-, two-, or three-story buildings surrounded by grounds that provide a garden-like setting.

Why do I focus on multifamily housing? People always need a place to live. If I have two options, having a home or an office, I go with a home first because I can work from home, but I can't make my home into an office. Because housing is a basic human need, investing in housing gives flexibility when the economy is soaring and when it's taking a nosedive. The rest of the economy might be turbulent, but because housing is a necessity, particularly for the workforce, it provides investment stability.

Contrast housing with office investments. If you invest in office or retail buildings and the national or local economy is poor, businesses won't rent space. During the 2007–2009 Great Recession, many retail spaces stood empty. E-commerce has been disrupting the traditional brick-and-mortar retail sector since the early 2000s. Mall occupancies continue to decrease, and anchor tenants like Sears and JCPenney are closing many stores. In 2017, Credit Suisse predicted that 20 to 25 percent of malls will close by 2022. Target and Walmart, stalwarts of the retail trade, are spending billions of dollars to make their stores and warehouses e-commerce friendly.

But even in a poor economy, people in the workforce work hard to keep their homes. Rents may not increase at a faster pace during those years, but most of the units will be occupied.

Understanding the Financial Structure of Real Estate Investing

Although the DNA of multifamily housing is similar to residential real estate, multifamily housing is commercial real estate because it operates as an investment that generates a profit. In both cases, however, loans from financial institutions enable buyers to purchase properties.

Much of the capital that finances multifamily housing is agency debt from Fannie Mae, Freddie Mac, and HUD. Fannie Mae and Freddie Mac are not government agencies; they are private companies that Congress chartered in 1938 and 1970, respectively. In contrast, HUD, the Department of Housing and Urban Development, is a government agency; its function is complicated, affected by political processes, and not relevant to the value-added business model we use, which is described later in this chapter. Major commercial lenders and other financial institutions also make loans for commercial real estate purchases.

The funds Fannie Mae and Freddie Mac loan are called "agency debt" because these financial institutions can borrow from the US Treasury, although there is no guarantee that the US Treasury must lend to them. In simplified terms, Fannie Mae and Freddie Mac buy mortgages from other lenders and guarantee that the principal and interest on those mortgages will be paid. The funds they supply when they purchase mortgages enable other financial institutions to make more loans. This buying and selling of mortgages creates a cycle that keeps the mortgage market liquid.

Loans come in two forms, recourse and nonrecourse. Individuals default on a recourse loan when they fail to make one or more payments on the principal and interest. In the case of default, the lender can recover its funds by taking possession of the borrower's asset, for example, by foreclosing on a home or repossessing a car. Often, the value of the asset does not cover the amount of funds remaining on the loan. With a recourse loan, the lender can recover the balance of the loan directly from the borrower.

Nonrecourse loans differ from recourse loans in two ways. First, the asset serves as collateral that guarantees the loan. In the case of commercial real estate, the collateral is the property you are borrowing to purchase. In the case of default, the lender can take the property and any cash flow it generates; usually, the value of the property and its cash flow covers the principal and interest on the loan. Second, a nonrecourse loan protects an individual's personal assets. If the value of the property and its cash flow are less than the principle and interest on the loan, the lender cannot recover the balance from you. The individual borrower bears less risk in this arrangement, and investors and the bank or financial institution bear greater risk. Because financial institutions bear greater risk, nonrecourse loans usually come with higher interest rates.

There are, however, conditions that protect the lender's interests. When these conditions are met, they provide the lender with the ability to recover the principal and interest on the loan directly from the borrower. Generally, these conditions, called "bad boy" carve outs, consist of unethical or illegal business practices. They include the following:

- Fraudulent financial reports or tax returns

- Overleveraging a property through additional financing (financing without the original lender's permission)

- Submitting financial reports or tax payments late

- Gross mismanagement

- Misrepresenting the property

- Damaging or destroying the property in a manner that decreases its value (for example, through arson)

- Voluntarily filing bankruptcy or conspiring to file bankruptcy[2]

Qualified properties and investors can get access to nonrecourse debt. Agency debt keeps the whole market liquid because the government backs the agencies. Other financial institutions provide nonrecourse loans to the multifamily industry as well.

To see the difference between recourse and nonrecourse loans, suppose you borrow $10 million through a recourse loan to buy an apartment complex or office space. If something goes wrong, you as the guarantor are liable. If there is a default for any of a multitude of reasons, the property would go into foreclosure and affect your personal liability and credit. Even if the reason for the default is a major economic meltdown, foreclosure and a negative impact on your credit still occur. In the multifamily industry, with Fannie Mae and Freddie Mac loans acting as a backbone and nonrecourse loans, you are not affected as an individual unless you commit gross mismanagement or fraud.

Why does it make more business sense to use nonrecourse loans than recourse loans? The answer is that nonrecourse loans provide noncontingent liability. And noncontingent liability gives you the

---

2   Blake Janover, "'Bad Boy' Carve-outs," Commercial Mortgage Quick Reference Guide, Multifamily loans, last accessed March 25, 2019, https://www.multifamily.loans/what-are-bad-boy-carve-outs.

John C. St. Janos, "Understanding the Scope of a Bad Boy Guaranty," *Herrick Publications* (blog), September 2017, http://www.herrick.com/publications/understanding-the-scope-of-a-bad-boy-guaranty/?utm_source=Mondaq&utm_medium=syndication&utm_campaign=View-Original.

James H. Schwarz and Linda A. Striefsky, "The Nuts and Bolts of Negotiating Nonrecourse Carve Outs (with Sample Provisions)," The Practical Real Estate Lawyer, January 2015, https://www.thompsonhine.com/uploads/1137/doc/Striefsky_-__Practical_Real_Estate_Lawyer.pdf.

ability to scale. When a bank evaluates a contingent loan, it looks at global cash flow, which includes the individual borrowing the funds. They will assess the person's liability against the person's income and reject the request to borrow if the person has too many liabilities. But in the case of nonrecourse loans, each property supports itself based on its cash flow (the bank calls this "debt service coverage ratio"). Because each property supports itself, you can get more than one loan. You can buy a lot more properties and scale your business. I have several properties financed through noncontingent liability nonrecourse loans at any particular time. Each property has a cash flow that supports itself (and generates a profit, which I'll talk about later), so no property affects my ability to get a new loan as long as I maintain a certain liquidity to qualify for the loan.

Financial institutions, however, don't just hand out loans for real estate investment deals. You must have some equity in the investment to make the deal happen. In the technology industry, start-ups raise seed money through venture capital. The money comes from private equity groups and individual investors. The start-up seeking venture capital must present a business plan and pitch to the investors. If they succeed in getting the venture capital and successfully launch the business, eventually they can have a public offering and raise further funding from selling bonds or shares of stock.

In commercial real estate, to close a multimillion-dollar deal, we must bring several million dollars to the table. Once the loan and the equity are in place, we buy the property. Most of the time we invest in properties that generate cash flow. If we underwrite the deal well and meet our performance expectations with efficient management, usually there is no need for further investment, no need to raise multiple rounds of capital, and no need for public offerings. The project sustains itself, generates a profit, and provides a service that people need. More than simply sustaining itself, paying for staff, the original debt, and taxes, the property pays a yield on the investment, and this is what makes it desirable to investors, like a stock or bond. Although other types of commercial real estate also pay a yield, multifamily deals are easier to execute because of the access to nonrecourse capital from financial institutions like Fannie Mae, Freddie Mac, and other commercial and bridge lenders.

Let's look at a case study. Suppose you are buying an apartment complex in the suburbs of Dallas, Texas, for $10,000,000. Financial institutions are willing to lend $6,500,000. The balance of $3,500,000 is the down payment or equity you must raise to acquire the property. An investment firm might put $2,450,000 into the deal, providing nearly 25 percent of the required capital or 70 percent of the down payment, and will do no more. But the deal is still short about $1,050,000. American Ventures has only so many funds available and typically invests 10 percent or more of the required equity capital or down payment. For the difference, I might call a group of friends, who then put in $100,000 to $250,000 each. This is called syndicating a deal and is a typical way to create a real estate investment opportunity. In a case like this, we create a single-purpose entity (SPE), typically a limited liability corporation (LLC), which acts as the entity that owns the asset. All the investors become members of the LLC, which protects their interests in the deal.

BECAUSE I FOCUS ON SCALING MY BUSINESS, I INVEST IN DEALS THAT HAVE TWO HUNDRED OR MORE UNITS.

The multifamily real estate industry thrives on nonrecourse financing. Because I focus on scaling my business, I invest in deals that have two hundred or more units. Eighty percent of my current commercial real estate (CRE) portfolio is in multifamily housing, and 20 percent is in land and other investments. To ensure adequate cash flow from the multifamily workforce housing, we try to invest in assets that can ideally be maintained at 90 percent and higher occupancy.

A Short Introduction to Investing in Land

A good percentage of my portfolio is in strategic land investments. One of my first land investments was on the east side of Austin, Texas. When I made that investment, I knew Austin was growing in that direction. What an investor can do with land in that area is wide open and depends on the size of the property. As development heads in that direction, we could create a townhouse community, an apartment community, or a mixed-use area, with housing, retail, and commercial buildings. If the land is big—multiple acres—and the city is ripe for it, an investor could create a master plan for a neighborhood.

I invested in East Austin in 2012 just before a stadium that hosts Formula 1 and US Grand Prix racing opened. I was confident the city was growing in that direction, the new stadium generated additional jobs, and the zoning restrictions were more relaxed; the area is in Austin's extraterritorial jurisdiction rather than within Austin city limits. I made two other investments in Austin where transit-oriented development zoning is in place, which gives developers density bonuses that typically don't exist for properties with different zoning ordinances. The biggest land investment I made was 101 acres in the city of Leander in north Austin, which is currently most suitable for dividing into one- to five-acre lots for single-family homes; with rapid growth, this land could become a master planned community.

Corporate Organization of a Multifamily Investment Firm

There are many ways to organize a firm that has larger investments—that is, multifamily residential properties with two hundred or more units—in its portfolio. A corporate team that manages the projects almost always consists of the acquisitions and asset management teams. There are two options for management of day-to-day activities, called property management: outsourcing to a third-party property management company or owning a property management company to keep that team in-house. For example, American Ventures had an in-house property management team for a couple of years. When we sold a lot of our existing assets, we exited that team. If in the future we maintain ownership of a few thousand units simultaneously, we are open to once again having a property management company that our asset management team would manage.

To choose the best organizational structure for your firm, it is important to understand each team's functions.

- **ACQUISITIONS TEAM.** Sources, underwrites, develops a business plan—consulting with the asset management team—negotiates, oversees due diligence, sources debt and equity, and closes the deal.

- **ASSET MANAGEMENT TEAM.** Provides input on business plans, participates in due diligence activities to get familiar with the property, and takes over from the acquisitions team at closing. They implement the business plan, including oversight of the capital improvements program and guiding the property management team on property operations. In addition, they communicate with lenders and investors, and prepare and submit reports to them.

- **CONSTRUCTION MANAGEMENT TEAM.** Assists in creating the initial capital improvement budget based on property tours and the business plan. They help inspect properties during due diligence, review the findings and estimates to fix deficiencies, and recommend adjustments to the capital improvement budget. Once the acquisition is complete, the team obtains and analyzes bids for capital improvements and oversees completion of the work.

- **PROPERTY MANAGEMENT TEAM.** Executes the business plan and manages day-to-day operations of the property. Their goals include leasing at maximum rates while keeping the property occupancy as high as possible and managing expenses to keep them as low as possible. They manage tenant relations and property upkeep to ensure residents are happy living at the property. They coordinate and communicate with the asset management team, and prepare and submit reports to them.

Whether you have property management in-house or outsourced depends on a variety of factors. Generally, when you own enough units in an area, an in-house property management team provides operational efficiencies that outsourcing cannot provide. In addition, you have greater control over the operations of the property management teams when they are in-house. However, property management tends to be a low-margin business. If you don't have a critical mass of units in an area, it is a money-losing endeavor, which negates the benefits you would see from in-house control.

How to Choose a Market for Your Investment

We started out asking how I ended up in Austin, Texas, when I was so in love with New York City. My background as a scientist leads to the answer again. When I decided to move there, careful observation and analysis led me to believe that the real estate market in Texas, which has the second largest economy in the country, offered opportunities for an emerging entrepreneur. Its population, jobs, per capita real gross domestic product, and per capita personal income are growing, and its economy is diversified. I noticed that four of the top ten metro economies are in Texas: Dallas, Houston, San Antonio, and Austin, all within two to four hours' driving distance. That's 40 percent of the best real estate markets in your backyard.

My research also identified commercial real estate as providing the best investment opportunity, and within that, multifamily real estate. Next, I identified the ability to access funds, particularly nonrecourse loans from agencies like Fannie May and Freddie Mac, to finance the deals.

Cash flow drives the entire industry, whether you are in New York, which is extremely expensive and volatile, or Dallas. One metric that serves as a starting place for decisions in the industry is the capitalization rate, usually shortened to cap rate. The cap rate compares net operating income (NOI) to the value of the property. Investors use the cap rate to begin evaluating real estate deals like they use price-to-earnings (P/E) ratios to begin evaluating stocks and stock-based investment instruments. Cap rates are the inverse of P/E ratios. Whereas a P/E ratio is price divided by earnings, a cap rate is earnings divided by price. Because earnings—net operating income—are static when you don't implement a value-add initiative, a cap rate tells you how expensive (price) those earnings are. When NOI is high and the price is low, the cap rate is high, and you are looking at a good opportunity. When NOI is low and price is high, the cap rate is low, and you should walk away from a low cap rate deal unless there is a tremendous risk-adjusted value-add potential.

To decide where to invest, we compare the cap rate in one area to the cap rate in another area. For example, let's say in New York properties are selling for 4 cap. At 4 cap, if you invest $100,000, you hope to get a 4 percent yield in earnings (NOI), which is $4,000. But in Dallas, suppose properties are selling for closer to 6 cap. At 6 cap, a $100,000 investment would generate $6,000 in earnings. Therefore, the yield on an investment is better in Dallas than in New York. This difference in cap rates was the situation when we were expanding our portfolio in Dallas.

Common ways to evaluate the investment decision in addition to cap rates are internal rate of return (IRR), multiple, and cash-on-cash yield during the hold time. These are not either-or methods of evaluating a deal; they each provide a different view of the same picture.

IRR takes into account both the total investment returns you make on a property (cash flow) and the amount of time it takes to achieve those returns. In the example of a $10,000,000 purchase price with $6,500,000 in debt and a cash investment of $3,500,000, if you sell the property after three years for $12,500,000, the resulting IRR is 24.6 percent. However, if you sell the property after five years for $12,500,000, the resulting IRR is 17.9 percent.

In contrast, the multiple ignores time. It is, simply, how much you multiplied your investment by. In this example, the cash investment is $3,500,000. Suppose, as before, you sell the property after five years for $12,500,000. After you repay the loan of $6,500,000, you have $6,000,000. If you received annual cash distributions of $275,000 for those five years, your total investment return is $3,875,000 (calculations below). Profits of $3,875,000 plus the return of your original investment of $3,500,000 equals $7,375,000. The multiple is $7,375,000 divided by $3,500,000, which equals 2.11.

A final metric is cash-on-cash returns. Using the same numbers, at 6 cap the NOI is $600,000 (NOI = cap rate × purchase price, so 6% × 10,000,000 = $600,000). If the interest rate on the loan is 5 percent, the debt service is $325,000. In this case, net income after debt service, which is also called cash flow or cash inflow, is $275,000. This $275,000 in cash inflow divided by the cash investment of $3,500,000, also called cash outflow, gives a cash-on-cash return of 7.86 percent.

How these metrics combine when evaluating a deal depends on several factors. If we are pursuing a heavy value-add deal, the cash-on-cash returns are typically lower at first, for example, 3 to 5 percent in year one. The cash-on-cash returns improve once the value-add is completed. For example, it increases to 5 to 8 percent in years two and three. In this case, investors are giving up some cash-on-cash returns. In exchange, they want to see a higher IRR for the deal, so they will scrutinize that value more carefully. On the other hand, if we are pursuing a more stabilized deal with less of a value-add component, investors will be willing to give up some of the higher IRR in exchange for a higher and more consistent cash-on-cash return from the beginning of the investment.

American Ventures's key performance indicator (KPI) for choosing a deal is a projected 20 percent IRR. Table 1, which follows, summarizes the calculations in this example.

TABLE 1: SUMMARY OF KEY METHODS FOR EVALUATING A DEAL

Purchase price	$10,000,000
Equity (cash outflow)	$3,500,000
Debt (loan)	$6,500,000
Debt service	$325,000 at a 5% yearly interest rate
Cap rate	6%
Net Operating Income	$600,000
Net income (cash inflow)	$275,000 ($600,000 – $325,000)
Cash-on-cash return	7.86% ($275,000 cash inflow / $3,500,000 cash outflow)
Sale price	$12,500,000
Internal Rate of Return after 3 years	24.6%
Internal Rate of Return after 5 years	17.9%

You also look at the economic factors at work in an area. At the big-picture level, you look at the key industries and population growth in an area, the ability to get loans, the interest rate on loans, and how the regional economy is performing.

At a more detailed level, we look into employment drivers, such as how many companies are moving into a region and how many jobs are being created there. We look at all the economic indicators: Are rents going up in this area? What is the job growth? What is the wage growth? How much investment is flowing into the region or a city like Dallas? We also investigate submarkets within a city using the same factors.

To assess a submarket, we look at whether it is in the city's growth path. We assess the schools and other social institutions. The city might have put resources into a growth path, upgrading the streets, sewer system, or other elements of infrastructure. Or we determine that growth is heading in that direction. For example, historically Austin has had a central downtown business district, but nearby outlying areas were not as developed. There are also areas, typically ranchland, where a lot of new construction—new homes and shopping malls—is happening, so between the central business district and its outlying areas lies the growth path. Residential assets in areas of the growth path, which were predominantly occupied by low-income people, are getting pushed farther out from the central business district. The areas just outside the central business district, which are predominantly occupied by people with low incomes, are becoming a little bit more median- to upper-income level as the city revitalizes neighborhoods or improves blighted regions. This pattern is called a path of gentrification, and it is where we find our best investment opportunities.[3]

In addition, the real estate industry establishes different generic categories that take into account the asset, its location, and the investment risk versus return. The categories range from Class A through Class C. Class A assets are relatively new—no older than fifteen years—

---

3   There is much debate about the effects of gentrification on neighborhoods. Some representative articles include:

John Buntin, "The Myth of Gentrification," Slate, January 14, 2015, https://slate.com/news-and-politics/2015/01/the-gentrification-myth-its-rare-and-not-as-bad-for-the-poor-as-people-think.html.

Poverty & Race Research Action Council, "Annotated Bibliography—Recent Literature on Gentrification, with an emphasis on policies to protect and benefit existing residents of gentrifying neighborhoods," PRRAC, September 2013, https://prrac.org/pdf/PRRAC_annotated_bibliography_on_gentrification_-_October_2013.pdf.

Rachel Bogardus Drew, "Gentrification: Framing Our Perceptions," Enterprise Community Partners, Inc., October 2018, https://www.enterprisecommunity.org/download?fid=10224&nid=7602.

upscale apartment high-rises or complexes with all the amenities in a great location; rent, tenants' incomes, and occupancy rates are all high. These assets don't produce a lot of cash flow, but they are very low risk: people who live there have good jobs, and their chance of defaulting on a rental payment is very low.

We buy B and C assets in B locations because they generate better return on investment. These are workforce residences in nice locations with rents that average-income people can afford. Class B assets tend to be older than Class A properties, and investors can implement a value-add program to renovate them. Class C properties may not have been kept up, which means that maintenance issues may exist, and they are likely older than twenty years; investors may have to renovate the building infrastructure to bring it up to code before implementing a value-add program. B and C assets may be safe, clean places to live, but the apartments don't have modern appliances, newly decorated interiors, and so on. But with rapid growth in an area and with additional capital expenditure by the current or a new owner, C properties can turn out to be Class B-minus or B assets.

A critical element in researching an area is to go there and observe, literally look around. Table 2 lists some of the questions to ask and how to evaluate the observations.

TABLE 2: HOW TO ASSESS A PROPERTY

QUESTIONS	INTERPRETING OBSERVATIONS
What is the physical condition of the property?	When major systems (roofs, siding, plumbing, HVAC, and so on) are in good condition, we can focus capital improvement dollars on upgrades and amenities that provide tangible value additions.
What do the cars in the parking lot look like? How many cars are in the parking lot?	A lot of cars in the middle of the day typically means most residents are service oriented, unemployed, underemployed, or retired.
How does the neighborhood look? How many and what kind of commercial properties are in the area? Are they beneficial to the residents (grocery, restaurants, retail, or medical)? Are there a lot of vacancies? What condition are these properties in?	Additional commercial properties in the immediate area increase a property's appeal, as residents don't have to travel far to access life necessities. Low vacancy and properties in good condition reflect strong market dynamics and a favorable investment environment.
In a residential area, how do the houses look? If they're older, are they well taken care of?	Pride of ownership in surrounding homes typically indicates a better and safer neighborhood and means you will attract a better tenant profile.
Are there parks nearby? Other recreational opportunities?	These amenities provide quality of life for residents and increase property values.
Is there a school nearby? If so, is it an elementary or high school?	Elementary schools typically have more attractive surroundings and less crime, and the opposite is true for high schools.
How is the access to the property? Are there nearby transportation opportunities, whether that's a train station, bus stops, or freeways? How far from employment sectors is the property?	If favorable, these conditions make a property more appealing to a larger demographic, thus increasing rental demand and values.

Other sources of information are data from commercial real estate information companies. CoStar, RealPage, Reis, and so on are online subscription services that provide statistics to help back up some of your intuitions from looking around. These data include market occupancies, rental rates, absorption rates (how quickly apartments are leased), construction pipeline, demographic reports, crime rates, and employment opportunities. These information sources also provide data such as who the current owner is and when the property was purchased. Knowing this information could give insight on market timing and the seller's motivation. A valuable source of information is a general Google search, which returns articles published by business journals. These provide information like "This quarter, ten new companies have moved into Dallas," which provides evidence of job growth. There are many sources of information that impact commercial real estate.

Metrics for Deals: Key Performance Indicators

When I put together a deal, I look at a few metrics, called key performance indicators (KPIs). When I was dealing with single-family homes, the KPIs were few and relatively simple. They included initial investment capital, cash flow during hold time, and net profit at exit. Before I would pursue a deal, I looked for current value of the property and after repair value by looking at comparable sales (comps) and rentals.

When I went from single-family to multifamily properties, the economies of scale created a lot more variables. Table 3 shows a spreadsheet I use, which I think every investor should use. The KPIs include equity multiple, which is how much equity increased (for example, a $100,000 investment that returns $200,000 is a multiple of 2), the acquisition cap rate, the current year and projected NOI, and the internal rate of return (IRR).

TABLE 3: CRE INVESTMENT KEY PERFORMANCE INDICATORS FOR DUNCANVILLE COMMONS

Units	300
Yr Built	1984

Purchase Price	$12,160,000
Purchase Price/ Unit	$40,533
IRR*	26.9%
Multiple	2.0x
Investor IRR	23.8%
Investor Multiple	1.8x
Cash-on-Cash Yr 1	15.7%
Cash-on-Cash Yr 2	16.7%
Cash-on-Cash Yr 3	13.3%

Loan Amount	$12,171,000
Equity Raise	$3,235,494
All In Cost	$15,406,494

Current Yr NOI§	$859,788
Yr 1 NOI	$1,159,483
Yr 2 NOI	$1,192,453
Yr 3 NOI	$1,282,893

Current Yr Rev	$2,141,568
Yr 1 Rev	$2,458,277
Yr 2 Rev	$2,530,211
Yr 3 Rev	$2,660,783

Current Yr OpEx**	$1,281,780
Yr 1 OpEx	$1,298,794
Yr 2 OpEx	$1,337,758
Yr 3 OpEx	$1,377,890

Rehab $	$2,608,984
Rehab $/Unit	$8,697
Rehab # Units	150
Rehab ROI†	10.5%
Acq Cap Rate‡	7.1%

Acq Cap Rate w/ Tax Adjust	6.6%
Acq Cap Rate Yr 1	9.5%
Acq Cap Rate Total Cost	5.6%
Acq Cap Rate Total Cost Yr 1	7.5%

In Place Rent	$639
In Place Rent $ /SqFt	$1.11
Post Rehab Rent	$716
Post Rehab Rent $/SqFt	$1.24
Incr / (Decr)	$76
Avg SqFt	576
Occupancy %	95.3%

Current Yr OpEx/unit	$4,273
Yr 1 OpEx/unit	$4,329
Yr 2 OpEx/unit	$4,459
Yr 3 OpEx/unit	$4,593

Closing Costs, Legal Fees, Etc.	$367,200
Acquisition fee	$121,600
Equity Acquisition Fee	$27,000
Loan Origination Fee	$121,710
Disposition Fee	$88,475

Current Prop Tax	$211,800
Prop Tax Yr 1	$272,620
Prop Tax Increase Yr 1	$60,820

Exit Cap Rate	7.25%
Sales Price	$17,695,070
Sales Price/Unit	$58,984

*IRR: Internal rate of return
†ROI: Return on investment
‡Acq Cap Rate: Acquisition capitalization rate
§NOI: Net operating income
**OpEx: operating expenses

In addition to building an underwriting model based on the KPIs, it is important to ask questions about them:

- What are the property taxes during our ownership? This is particularly important in Texas where the property tax rates are around 2 to 3 percent of value depending on which county the property is located in. Texas is a nondisclosure state, meaning there is no requirement to disclose how much a property is sold or bought for. When a purchase is made, the county may adjust the property taxes on its next annual appraisal, which can increase the taxes by thousands or millions of dollars. So we always underwrite the deal with higher property taxes as if the new assessed value of the property is close to 85 to 95 percent of our purchase price.

- How much in capital investments are you making per door (that is, per unit), and what is the return on equity for those dollars?

- What are the operating expenses per door? Is the property being run efficiently or are there opportunities to reduce operating expenses and thus raise NOI?

- What is your projected increase in revenue from rent or your potential exit sales price? Do market comps support this amount?

Internal rate of return (IRR) is a critical KPI. At American Ventures, we distinguish ourselves from other firms by setting a very high bar for IRR. For example, if a deal doesn't have an IRR in the high teens or low twenties over three to five years of hold time, then we don't have a high interest in pursuing the deal. In 2014 through 2017, we targeted 20 percent IRR deals. We might evaluate fifty deals, short-list only five to evaluate further, and buy only one or two of them because only those two meet the IRR metric. The key to achieving the 20-plus percent IRR goal is being systematic about evaluating the projects and only going after properties that meet this criterion. In the current real estate market, a 20 percent IRR is like a home run. The more deals we engage in, however, the fewer we can find with that kind of IRR.

Although investors are mainly interested in IRR or ROI, what is more important to us is the cap rate at the time of acquisition. Because the cap rate takes NOI and the purchase price into account, it is a good measure of value. Right now, in New York multifamily properties sell for 3 to 4 percent cap. But in Dallas similar properties sell for 5.5 or 6 percent cap. We were able to buy off-market properties in 2014 at a low to middle 6 percent cap. When you buy, you want to buy at a higher cap rate—this means the NOI is high. But when you sell, you want to sell at a low cap. Recall that the cap rate is NOI divided by the purchase price. Once you buy a property, the purchase price is locked; it cannot change. But NOI can change, and you always want it to increase over the time that you hold a property. When NOI increases, the cap rate also increases.

Let's look at a specific example. The deal described in Table 3 is a value-added deal, and the key financial metrics are on the left. We struck a purchase price of $12,160,000 with the seller. However, going into the deal, we knew we wanted to invest $2,608,984 in renovating and stabilizing the property—the value added—which made the total cost a little over $15,400,000 (including legal and other fees). We were able to get bank funding for a little over $12,000,000.

This property needed to be a value-added deal because, although the property was doing well—it was 90 percent occupied—the previous owner didn't upgrade it. Buildings in the surrounding area were improved, but the owner of this property left it alone. As a result, for example, the owner of the property next door could charge $125 more for the same 576-square-foot unit as this property. The unit in the property next door looks better when you walk inside because it has better flooring, better countertops, better appliances, and so on.

When we buy a property that has not been similarly renovated, like Duncanville Commons, we do a lot of exterior work, such as painting—including the clubhouse—and improving the amenities. We also do interior unit renovations, for example, two-tone paint, granite countertops, good flooring (the trend right now is simulated wood laminate flooring; it looks beautiful and is easy to maintain), good light fixtures (the current trend is pendant lighting), and up-to-date appliances. After completing renovations, we sometimes give the complex a new name if the prior name is less appealing. A fresh and new name is important when we need to rebrand apartment complexes that might have had a bad reputation or poor reviews.

After renovating the property, we can increase the rent to the going market rate. All that renovation has a cost that needs to be included in the deal from the outset. For this property, we put close to $8,700 per unit into renovations. Generally, renovation costs per door run from $5,000 to $10,000, but they can be more on some deals.

After doing a few value-added deals like this, an investment idea crossed our minds. Most operators of value-added deals, apart from renovating the exterior of the property, renovate 100 percent of the interior units, hoping to capture increased rents on all the renovated units. Our unique idea was to renovate the interiors of only 50 percent of the units in a property and leave the potential— "meat on the bone"—for our buyer, in turn, to add value. That way we create a chain of value-added deals starting with us and extending to our buyers.

When we upgrade only 50 percent of a property, we reduce the renovation budget and overall cost of investment. Therefore, our return on investment is greater than if we had renovated 100 percent of the units; we have strong data to support this result.

When we are ready to sell, we capture a wide range of buyers—buyers who are interested in less risk so accept lesser returns, and buyers who are interested in taking a deal to the next level so accept greater risk. Buyers willing to realize lower returns for lower risk are open to paying a premium for our deal. Then they hold the property for cash flow.

Alternatively, buyers can implement a value-add program on the remaining units and get higher returns. Because there are internal higher-rent comparables within the property, renovating and increasing the rent on the remaining 50 percent of the units is a low-risk venture. Buyers pursuing a value-add deal don't have to reinvent the business plan.

If you look back at the spreadsheet, you'll see that we borrowed about $12,000,000, but knew we needed about $15,400,000 to execute the deal. The additional $3,400,000 can come from different sources. That is, there are different ways of buying a property. If I had the $3,400,000 myself, I would create a limited liability corporation (LLC)—which protects my personal assets—and simply buy the property. But if I have only $3,400,000, I can buy only one property, and I cannot scale my business. If I invest $340,000 of my own capital and raise the balance of $3,060,000 from investors instead, I can potentially spread my $3,400,000 over ten different properties.

And that is what American Ventures LLC does. AV puts 10 percent of the equity capital into an investment. We raise the remaining capital from private equity groups, family offices, and high-net-worth individuals. While most of the private equity groups and family offices are sophisticated and play an active role in investments, a majority of high-net-worth individuals want to participate in real estate investment but don't know how. AV participates in joint ventures with all investor groups.

The Operating Agreement

AV is accountable to the investors for a project's performance, and each investor takes a different approach to involvement in a project. Some are silent partners, and some are hands on, talking to us every month to monitor progress. Institutional investors tend to be hands on, while high-net-worth investors have their own full-time jobs so tend to be silent partners. AV is always the managing member, does the day-to-day work involved in a project, and works hand in hand with property management companies. In an LLC structure, AV acts as a managing member while the investors are called members and don't get involved in operational issues. Managing members can also be called sponsors or operators of the deal.

With multiple investors in a project, determining how to organize the corporation and share the cash flow is a high priority. When we put together a real estate investment deal, before we acquire a property and while we are doing the due diligence, we launch a single-purpose entity (SPE) or vehicle (SPV), typically an LLC, which is governed by an operating agreement or company agreement that everyone must follow. Each member of the investment deal is an "owner" of the property and has roles and responsibilities, just like any other LLC. AV has fiduciary duties and so do all the other people who own the property. We also have various management duties and typically charge 1 percent of the gross revenue as an asset management fee; 1 percent coming from several projects ends up being a substantial sum to run day-to-day operations of the corporate team. But AV is not in the game to earn fees. Rather, we put together the deal to earn good profits for our investors, who can include private equity groups, family offices, or individual investors, and in turn earn a share of profits based on performance. This performance-driven returns model is crucial; as investors earn more profits, so does AV.

The operating agreement specifies all the details of the SPE and how a property's cash flow is shared among the partners. How much of the cash flow a partner gets depends on the percentage of capital they contributed to the deal at the outset. The operating agreement spells out how members make equity contributions, how the SPE maintains capital accounts, how it makes distributions, how it allocates profits and losses, and how it structures tax allocations.

Although sharing cash flow and profits are critical details, other aspects of the operating agreement are equally important. It lays out the responsibilities of the managing member, limits on its authority, and how the entity makes major decisions. The agreement also details the members' responsibilities and limitations on their actions. It determines the fees paid to the managing member for acquisition, asset management, construction management, and disposition of the asset. Importantly, the agreement details how the members terminate and dissolve the entity.

Threats and Risks

UNFORESEEN THREATS

Some threats are unforeseen, and not because you overlooked some piece of information. American Ventures's goal is to expand into select primary, secondary, and tertiary markets in the United States. So far, we have invested in most of the primary markets of Texas, but as part of our strategic expansion program, we also short-listed a couple of secondary and tertiary markets. Weather is perhaps the biggest threat that you cannot predict. For example, we went into the Corpus Christi market with a plan to invest in five hundred fifty rental units across two apartment complexes. We brought in one of the big national private equity groups to invest in the deal. We identified Corpus Christi as a growth area because of port expansion, among many other

WEATHER IS PERHAPS THE BIGGEST THREAT THAT YOU CANNOT PREDICT.

factors. The port in Corpus Christi now sends crude oil to India and China, two big countries that have expanding economies. We made a smaller acquisition and planned to make a larger acquisition. This larger acquisition was a property on the bay and the main reason we were investing in the Corpus Christi market. Ten days before this bigger acquisition, Hurricane Harvey caused close to two million dollars in damage to the property. We ended up letting the deal go. You cannot predict some things, and the effects of weather are a big one.

Hurricane Harvey, a severe weather event that lasted seventeen days and caused $125 billion in damage, was devastating. Our portfolio has close to four hundred units across two apartment complexes in Lake Jackson, which is close to Houston, where Hurricane Harvey hit. Consequently, we took longer to implement our business plan. Based on projections, we should have sold the property in late 2018. But to get our projected returns, our current plan is to hold on to the property, stabilize it, and sell in 2019. The property took a big occupancy dip because of the hurricane. This risk was unpredictable, but we were able to use time to effectively mitigate the hurricane's effects.

We've looked at two ways to deal with unpredictable risks: cancel a deal or change the business plan to reduce the effects. Another way to mitigate risks is by having good insurance policies in place.

PREDICTABLE RISKS

Unlike weather, you can predict other risks. And when you can predict a risk and observe downsides, you can make a plan to deal with them. Rather than reacting to an unforeseen event, you are taking a proactive stance toward a foreseen factor. We evaluate these risks, also called deal killers, by stress testing the underwriting model during the acquisition process. The stress testing makes sure that the deal is still worth pursuing if any of these risks occur. The factors we evaluate and how we evaluate them include interest rate increases, cap rate increases, rent decreases, renovation capital expenditure increases, and fluctuations in occupancy, among others.

- **INTEREST RATE INCREASES:** If you have a floating-rate loan and, let's say, if current rates are at 5 percent, is it still a good deal if rates go up to 6 percent? What about 7 percent?

- **CAP RATE INCREASES:** If you project to sell the property at a 5 percent cap rate based on current market conditions that make the deal work, what happens if cap rates end up being 5.5 percent in a particular market? What about 6 percent? Is your sales price still enough to make the returns you need?

- **RENTAL RATES:** If you think you will be able to charge $200 more for rent based on your renovation plan, what happens if you can only charge $150 more?

- **RENOVATION COSTS:** If you project spending $5,000 per door on interior renovations, what happens if, after putting together a detailed budget, the cost ends up running $5,500 per door? Do you still achieve the forecasted return on investment (ROI) you need to make the deal work?

- **FLUCTUATIONS IN OCCUPANCY:** When investing in markets

that depend on specific companies or industries, like petrochemical plants in Corpus Christi, what happens to occupancy when a plant initiates an end-of-year furlough or layoff? What happens to occupancy at a property next to a military base, like Fort Hood, following a sudden deployment? What impact do rapid fluctuations in occupancy have on forecasted income?

Scanning the Environment for Future Opportunities

In addition to these kinds of analyses, I keep informed about what else is big and what else is coming up two or three years down the road. By asking questions on these issues, I discovered qualified opportunity zones (QOZs). A QOZ is an economically distressed and low-income area that the governor of each state designates. The 2017 tax cut created the investment incentive, and President Trump signed an executive order near the end of 2018 to support the program with federal funds. The goal is to spur development through private sector investment in areas impacted by poverty and geographic inequality.[4] Every state has designated opportunity zones, and there are almost nine thousand across the country. New federal tax reforms provide the incentive for developing these distressed areas. With the new tax code in place, government agencies are developing guidelines that will defer or eliminate the federal taxes on capital gains if you invest in QOZs before the end of 2019.

Why is this a good deal? Let's say the capital gain on a real estate

---

4   Jim Tankersly, "Trump to Steer More Money to 'Opportunity Zones,'" *The New York Times*, December 12, 2018, https://www.nytimes.com/2018/12/12/us/politics/trump-opportunity-zones-tax-cut.html.

investment would be $100,000 under the old tax code. I can invest the $100,000 into land in an opportunity zone and hold that asset. I can then build a property on that land for another $100,000 to increase the basis by two times in the next thirty months and hold it long-term. Reductions in capital gain taxes occur after five and seven years (10 percent reduction in capital gains taxes on the original $100,000 profit after five years and 5 percent additional reduction after seven years). But after holding that asset for ten years, my new capital gains on that investment are completely tax free. Let's say I can sell this property in year ten and after for $500,000. This means that the initial $200,000 investment ($100,000 to purchase the land and $100,000 to build) created a capital gain of $300,000. The new tax code completely cancels the tax on that capital gain.

The window to take advantage of QOZ investments closes before the end of 2019 but may be extended. If we are aware of the opportunity and have a way to act on it, doing so creates an instant boost. The basis of the investment is much lower. For example, I might usually invest only $60,000 to $70,000 instead of $100,000 because of the tax burden. In QOZs, I can invest the entire $100,000 and get a better return on it.

Only about 20 percent of the commercial real estate business knows about QOZs and how they work. Although AV is aware of them, we are doing more research to pin down the details. But we are ahead of 80 percent of the competition.

THE ABILITY TO SEE TWO TO THREE YEARS IN ADVANCE IS A CRITICAL ELEMENT OF SUCCESS.

The ability to see two to three years in advance is a critical element of success. When we consider investing in a market, we first look into the employment drivers. Who is hiring in this area? Which companies are moving in; which are moving out? What is the strength of the local economy? What are the details of the market? How much are rents increasing? Employment drivers, economic indicators, what is happening at the microsubmarket level—these are all fundamental factors to research and develop insight into. For example, Dallas is the fourth largest metropolitan area in the United States. Each area within that larger metropolitan area has pockets of submarkets. Our analysts research the fundamentals in each of these submarkets, as well as the larger Dallas market. Our analysts also collect a lot of data on a property. Each analyst has a pipeline of perhaps ten good-looking deals. Then we might have twenty deals to review. Typically, we hold on to a property for three to five years. The goal is to make a good cash flow while we are holding the property. Analyzing the fundamentals is what enables us to choose the properties that represent the greatest opportunities for a good return.

The basic factors that help us spot future opportunities are demographic trends and trends in how people live. There are two significant demographic factors at work in the housing industry right now. One is the lifestyle choices of millennials.[5] They tend to prefer living in urban centers and having the flexibility to move from one place to another. However, rent is high in urban centers, and younger millennials carry a significant amount of student loan debt. The proportion of their income going to rent and to pay off debt makes it difficult for them to save enough to purchase a home.[6] People in this age group reflect about 40 percent of the working-age population, and their choices are likely to have an impact on housing for about the next thirty years.

---

5   Krista Franks Brock, "How Millennial Lifestyles Impact Homeownership," *Daily Dose* (blog), MReport, July 9, 2018, https://themreport.com/daily-dose/07-09-2018/millennial-lifestyles-impact-homeownership-rates.

6   Jeff Andrews, "Why aren't millennials buying houses?" *Affordable Housing* (blog), Curbed, July 11, 2018, https://www.curbed.com/2018/7/11/17541364/why-arent-millennials-buying-houses.

The other big demographic trend is retiring baby boomers. Every day in the United States, about ten thousand people turn sixty-five.[7] This trend is driving an increase in the need for fifty-five-plus and senior housing and will continue to do so through 2030.[8]

Every deal is different, and so are the KPIs. The properties need different degrees of renovation or no renovations at all, the operating agreement is different, and the threats and risks are different. But one thing is the same across all deals. You must always stick to the basics: systematic research, a systematic look at the data, systematic analysis, and a systematic implementation of the business plan. When you stick to the basics and are systematic about it, you have the best chance of investing in a good deal.

7   Adam Bergman, "Social Security Feels Pinch as Baby Boomers Clock out for Good," *Great Speculations* (blog), *Forbes*, June 21, 2018, https://www.forbes.com/sites/greatspeculations/2018/06/21/social-security-feels-pinch-as-baby-boomers-clock-out-for-good/#3b68daf44995.

8   Patrick Sisson, "The Changing Face of Retirement: Apartment Living, Active Lifestyles, and Rural Homes," *Property Lines* (blog), *Curbed*, May 22, 2018, https://www.curbed.com/2018/5/22/17380204/baby-boomers-retirement-senior-housing.

EXECUTIVE SUMMARY

- Choose an industry to work in that fully engages your interest, curiosity, and passion.

- Learn the industry by working in it at the simplest level first.

- Systematically analyze what you learn to identify how the industry meshes with people's basic needs. Find a gap between what people need and what the industry offers. Systematically analyze that gap to find a way to innovate to fill it.

- Know your industry's key performance indicators, learn how to measure them—both qualitatively and quantitatively—and use them to analyze and evaluate every opportunity you engage in.

- Identify and analyze the risks. Divide the risks into predictable risks and unpredictable risks. Use key performance indicators to mitigate predictable risks. Use time and insurance to mitigate unpredictable risks.

- Systematically scan all aspects of the environment, analyze what you learn, and use that information to identify opportunities before the competition does.

CHAPTER 3

TEAM AND TALENT

The critical elements of making a deal are to know all aspects of your industry, understand the key performance indicators (KPIs), and apply this knowledge systematically. An implicit element of a deal is to structure it in a way that benefits all the parties. All these elements come into play when you scale up your business and need to partner with others.

When I started investing in real estate while I still had a day job, I worked hard to learn the industry. We all have strengths and weaknesses. I focused on my strengths and hired team members whose strengths are my weaknesses. For me, TEAM is an acronym for Together, Everyone Accomplishes More. To make this motto a reality, we developed KPIs, and we had well-stated, measurable objectives.

When my focus was investing in single-family homes, I knew I had blind spots and weak areas. Even though these were small deals—fix-and-flip or fix-and-hold single-family homes—I knew I needed an expert partner, at least on one or two deals. I spotted my expert when

I saw an advertisement for a course on zero-down real estate investing. At $10,000, the course was too expensive for me. So I contacted the man running it and said, "I know you believe in your course so much that you charge $10,000 to take it. There's no doubt that it's well worth it. But I can't use my savings from my day job to pay you; it's too much up-front risk." Then I asked him, "Can you partner with me on the first two or three deals, and we'll share the profits?" He said, "No, I don't partner with anyone. I only teach my courses." But maybe he saw something in me, because after a week he called back and asked me to meet him for lunch. He taught me some basics, which helped me refine what I was doing. But he was an expert on one subject, and I was ready to do more.

The important lesson here is that you must know your strengths and weaknesses, work to your strengths, and find partners or employees who are skillful in your weak areas.

TEAM: Together, Everyone Accomplishes More

Structure situations so that benefit accrues just as much to your team as to you and your business partners. When you are starting with limited capital, just as you cannot start a commercial real estate project without investors, you cannot approach investors if you don't have a good team working with you. You really can't get anywhere without a good team: a team with talent, with strengths that complement your strengths and fill in the gaps of your weaknesses. Your goal is to create a win-win situation for the team, the board of directors, the founder or owner, and above all, the investors.

Talent is so important that it is a theme that runs through the sections that follow. But what is talent? Most people think that individuals are born with a talent—it's often called a gift. Yes, on the surface, it's something that is natural or built in, but talent is much more than that. To me, talent combines interest in a field and the willingness to let that interest drive you to put time and effort into pursuing excellence. In sports, we often think of someone being born with an ability. Michael Phelps is a good example. During the 2016 Summer Olympics,

TALENT COMBINES INTEREST IN A FIELD AND THE WILLINGNESS TO LET THAT INTEREST DRIVE YOU TO PUT TIME AND EFFORT INTO PURSUING EXCELLENCE.

sports analysts said that he has a perfect body for championship swimming. But if he did not train, practice, and challenge himself with competition, he would not have won twenty-three Olympic gold medals. It is the same with an intellectual pursuit or a career. You have talent when you let your interests drive you to excel.

WHAT KIND OF TEAM DO YOU WANT?

The key to knowing what kind of team you want and what kind of team you need—these may not be the same—is understanding your strengths and weaknesses. Understanding your strengths and weaknesses entails a certain amount of self-analysis, the same as evaluating your company's strengths and weaknesses involves a deep look at the company. There are no books to read, no workshop or guidance that will help you. You must dig in to discover and own your strengths and uncover and equally own your weaknesses. Only then can you find the necessary qualities in other people, successfully hire them, and help them grow into a well-functioning team. Developing this awareness requires the same kind of systematic research that you use to understand the industry you work in. A main difference, but not the only difference, is that your attention is turned inward rather than outward.

"It doesn't make sense to hire smart people and tell them what to do; we hire smart people so they can tell us what to do." Steve Jobs wrote these words in 2011, and I never tire of hearing them or reading them, no matter how often people repeat them. What did Jobs mean by "smart people"? I think it means people, from the top of your company to the bottom, who have strengths and weaknesses that complement each other.

For example, if I want to grow my multifamily real estate investment firm, I want to have an amazing person doing acquisitions—acquisitions are the core of what we do. All they do is analysis and acquisitions, buying properties. Their strength is finding those properties, analyzing them, and buying them. If I hire an amazing acquisitions person, why would I then say to them, "You can't do this. Do that instead"? The talented acquisitions person should be able to figure out what to do and guide you to the best deals. Once the acquisitions person tells you that a deal is good and the company should go after it, you review it to cross-check, because it's your bottom line. But their talent and role are finding and underwriting the deals, and your role is to enable them to do that.

Once you buy properties, someone—an asset manager—must manage them. After the analyst comes up with the model, analysis, and forecast, year after year the baton passes to the asset manager, who must manage the properties to meet the expectations laid out in the forecast. We must have an equally competent asset manager, someone who has managed and turned properties around, someone with a huge track record. You don't want the asset manager treating your properties as guinea pigs. He or she must have the experience and must be on board during the analysis and acquisitions phase, aware of the KPIs, and ready for the handoff.

The need for a top-notch asset manager was not obvious to me at the outset. Even though we were tremendously successful on quite a few deals, we also failed on a few deals. Looking back at those failures, I recognize that we hired a couple of people who were not competent. The properties they managed struggled. By the time we realized the problem, it took a long time for those properties to recover and begin to generate the planned cash flow.

The phrase *smart people* is generic. To me, *smart* means experience and talent. And experience and talent come at a cost. As I learned, however, a lack of experience and talent also has a cost. So I always want to devote resources to finding, hiring, and motivating experienced and talented people.

HIRE PEOPLE—EVEN A MENTOR—WHOSE STRENGTHS ARE YOUR WEAKNESSES

In an entrepreneurial venture, there must be two roles at the top. One person specializes in vision and strategy. That's the person who comes up with great ideas. Complementing great ideas, there has to be great execution. When I do my self-analysis, I know I have a couple of strengths and maybe ten weaknesses. The question I ask myself is "How do I partner with someone whose strengths are my weaknesses?" For success, it is critical that you partner or hire to your weaknesses. You need to work with people whose strengths are your weaknesses and whose weaknesses are your strengths. You should create this complementary situation through talent, interests, and experience. To find and buy the best deals, the combined experience of the team should be about fifty-plus years, if not more.

The simple example that comes to mind is Larry Page and Sergey Brin of Google. They brought Eric Smith in as CEO of the company because they had all the engineering skills, the ideas, the strategy, and the execution, but they needed someone with the experience and tested skills—someone who has been there and done the work—to lead.

When I was starting out buying single-family homes and selling them, before I scaled, my activity was learning by doing. Many entrepreneurs start this way, and that's an okay approach when your company is just you. However, when you get into a scaled-up company, you don't want the executive team to learn by doing. The stakes are too high, and that's why you hire experience for executive roles. When you're playing with your own money, learning by doing is fine. When you're dealing with a scaled-up business, you're playing with your and others' money, and learning by doing is no longer appropriate.

> **WHEN YOU GET INTO A SCALED-UP COMPANY, YOU DON'T WANT THE EXECUTIVE TEAM TO LEARN BY DOING.**

Near the beginning of my single-family home venture, when I was doing smaller deals, I realized that if I wanted to reach my goals, I needed to draw on someone with expertise beyond my own. As I described at the beginning of the chapter, I partnered on the first one or two deals with a real estate industry expert. I did the legwork, and he provided mentoring, telling me what to do and what not to do. I needed only a couple of months of mentoring like this before I became confident in what I was doing.

He taught me some basics, but I found other ways of creating deals. I could try different methods and learn because it was on a very small scale, and I was playing only with my money and 100 percent or 103 percent loans from banks (remember, I borrowed the purchase price and a little more to add value to the home).

After several extremely successful ventures in the single-family industry, I wanted to accomplish more through bigger investments in multifamily and commercial real estate and economies of scale. Through coinvesting and joint ventures, American Ventures offers institutional investors, private equity firms, family offices, and accredited investors access to quality multifamily and CRE investment opportunities. We quickly grew to a few thousand units across multiple properties and successfully exited several deals. As I prepare to take the next leap and scale up American Ventures to a billion-dollar real estate company, I will look up to mentors and industry leaders to teach me about moving from the scale of my current business to the next stage. We are positioned to more than double our portfolio with a planned pipeline of acquisitions slated to close in 2019 through 2020. I'm looking at the biggest developers, someone who has worked at Blackstone, for example, to identify these mentors. In fact, I know that I need two or three mentors, each one serving his or her purpose.

Incentivizing Talent

Motivating people—I mean providing the right incentives—is just as important as hiring the right people. With the right incentives in place, people focus on their positions, rather than, say, looking for another job. Cutting corners by hiring people at a lesser salary leads to failure; in fact, you can trace 23 percent of small business failures to having the wrong team.[9] With a higher salary as an incentive, you get a higher quality person, and then that higher salary keeps them focused on their work.

When the incentive—the salary—is lower, you end up hiring someone with less experience and less talent. And most of the time, when you pursue that strategy, two things happen. The person you

---

9   Rose Leadem, "Five reasons why businesses fail (infographic)," *Entrepreneur*, July 1, 2017, https://www.entrepreneur.com/article/296491.

hire learns while doing, which has a cost, and looks around for a job with a higher salary, which means he or she is not as focused. This all results from not having the right incentives in place.

We hire people who will work hard and then reward them for their hard work through bonuses, in this case a percentage of the deal. Every time we sell a deal, we distribute a set percent of the profits to the key people who put together and managed the deal. A set percent doesn't seem large, but they all add up across multiple properties. Typically, we incentivize the team at the time of acquisition and when we sell. For example, let's say we made one million dollars' profit on a deal. Five percent of that is $50,000. So the acquisitions analyst who helped find and underwrite the deal, who did all the legwork, gets a set percent. A director of acquisitions might get a little higher percent of the profit. Asset managers get a percent of the deal returns. The junior-level people who help make a deal may get a little lower than senior-level executives. They all must be employed in the company when we sell the property and realize the profit for them to realize the bonuses.

In a year when we are making, let's say, $5 million, these percentages add up. Five percent is about $250,000. For us, the talent matters more than how old a person is. We have a millennial in our office, barely twenty-three years old, and she will make a six-figure income for the first time because she gets a set percent of ten deals. These incentives are meaningful for people, and they help us retain the best people.

In addition to this financial incentive structure, we have standard benefits like health insurance and perks like free lunch every Friday from Uber Eats or the latest on-trend restaurant. When we buy and sell a deal, we shut down the office for two or three hours and go out for an event. Every quarter we have team-building events; we go to

Topgolf, which is a big golfing-plus-restaurant area, or we go to Punch Bowl, which has bowling lanes with a big restaurant and many other things to do. Buying or selling a deal calls for a team event. We also have quarterly and yearly team meetings at an outside location.

Building Your Team: How to Find Talented and Experienced People

Talent is essential whether you are less experienced or more experienced—it's a pivotal criterion for us. If you have talent but no experience, the question becomes whether you are willing to start off as an intern with a low cost to the company. And if you have talent but no experience, are you willing to learn and grow?

Learning and growing with us is essential, so we offer our employees educational benefits by covering the cost of certification or management courses. For example, one of our maintenance staff in our San Antonio buildings took a pool maintenance certification course. We also sponsored one of our asset managers to earn his Certified Property Manager (CPM) designation from the Institute of Real Estate Management; the CPM focuses on ethical leadership and signifies that a property is well managed. Taking a certification course is optional, but this individual went above and beyond the minimum. We recognized him at the company party because we put a high value on this kind of initiative. When I see this drive to excel, I know I am seeing someone who is talented. It is that quality of letting yourself be driven to excel—being willing to put in the extra effort—that we value so highly.

Internships are mainly for people still in college. They're in their final year and ready to graduate. We start them at twenty to thirty hours a week and work around their school schedule. If they perform, then by the time they graduate, if they're willing, we offer them a full-time position.

This approach is not without risk. For example, one of our full-time employees was enrolled in a full-time MBA program—that is, not an executive MBA program that holds courses on the weekends and online. Working full-time and engaging in a full-time MBA program is a huge workload, so we were flexible and enabled him to work around his course schedule. Being flexible was easy because he had experience and lots of talent; he single-handedly ran many deals. After he graduated, I was not able to hire him immediately because we were watching our balance sheet. Consequently, we could not retain him. A big company gave him almost double the salary, and he moved on with his life.

Another option is hiring people short-term without putting them on a payroll; instead, you bring them on as a consultant. This strategy often meshes with a situation when you need additional help during a busy time but maybe not in the near future. At the outset, you need to make it clear whether once there is more opportunity in the company you will convert the consultant to a full-time employee. Bringing someone on as an intern or consultant is a way to assess their talent and how well they learn without incurring costs.

There is a downside to this strategy for getting to know somebody without incurring huge costs. It comes with the risk that the person will not give 100 percent to the company because they don't know whether the company is where they want to work. Nevertheless, it is a strategy for being cautious and managing the risk of hiring.

It is no surprise that finding talented and experienced people mirrors how people find good jobs. They look for open positions in their fields on job boards and network to access the hidden job market.

I use two main ways to hire the right people. In the first, I simply place an ad for a position on a job board like Indeed.com. Because there is no cost to placing an ad and no cost to job seekers, you get hundreds of résumés. Even so, I'm sure I'm missing out. Despite that, when you get 120 résumés, you can comb through them and find five that are outstanding.

In the other, I use my network. I tell my peers in the industry that I'm looking to fill a position and ask, "Who could be the right guy? Who could be the right fit?" But asking around is a lot of work because you may come across someone or you may not. It's almost like dating. Finding a good person and letting their friend introduce you is a random event. And you can waste your time: you can take two months to find a potential candidate, only to learn they already have a job that they are happy with.

A friend recommended a third option—working with specialist recruiters. When I thought about it, this option seemed the same as going through a broker to buy and sell properties. The brokers weed out the best prospects for a deal. Working with an intermediary comes with a cost because doing the legwork is their job, but when you use a recruiter—a job broker, so to speak—they do the work of finding candidates and you can focus on your business.

Enabling the Best Employees to Do the Best Job

To get the best performance out of very talented and experienced people, you must give them access to everything they need to do a good job. This starts with providing an amazing office space to work in so that people look forward to coming to work every day. People need to be fully empowered to do their best work, and a lively workplace with good office space supports this. We want team members who really look forward to coming to work with zeal and passion every day.

Once you provide good office space, you need to provide people with all the right tools; every industry has many tools for doing the work. For example, in our company every desk has a laptop that connects to multiple monitors. We provide access to data services: CoStar, LoopNet, Smart Apartment Data, and a few others. The analysts develop specialized underwriting and forecasting models; each deal is unique, so building your own model makes more sense than buying a model. We just implemented the IMS software platform across all our deals to streamline business practices and provide transparency to investors. Property managers use software like Entrata and Yardi to facilitate processes like maintenance requests, new residents moving in, renewals, and so on.

Creating a good company culture is just as important as providing a great workspace and great tools. We are a small team, so everyone's goal is the same. There is no office politics. Office politics leads to a toxic environment; allowing that is not worth it. The ability to rule out office politics comes from taking a lot of time to hire and immediately firing if it becomes necessary. Having a zero-tolerance policy for a toxic work environment is easier to do with a small team—only about six people at any time—than in a big organization that has hundreds of employees.

Another aspect of having a small team is that it is easy to foster open communication. Unless someone is taking an important call, everyone's door is open. If someone needs to have a longer conversation and a deeper discussion, we all set time in advance.

At the time of writing, we own a property management company that has 150-plus employees. In organizations like that, you need an equally massive culture. To create that culture, we have a person on the team with experience in operations and managing a large staff. This is also a good example of matching weaknesses and strengths. My strength is structuring and closing deals, so I teamed up with people who have expertise in operations management.

To enable top talent to do their best work, we have great working conditions, team up people so that strengths and weaknesses complement each other—even in top management—have a no-politics policy, and have transparent communication.

Communication

Earlier I talked about the central role the acquisitions team plays. Essentially, the acquisitions team members spend time looking for deals. How they communicate about those deals is just as important as finding them.

First, they create a pipeline of deals. They underwrite each deal and make sure they fill the pipeline with all the details. They regularly evaluate the deals in the pipeline and sort them into good, better, and best categories. Then they will let me know that they want to talk about a deal, and we will spend time on it.

The deal includes the underwriting model and, if a broker is involved, a package of information from the broker. We have a conversation in which the acquisitions team shows me the deal, what it looks like, the number of units, the underwriting model, and the pluses and minuses. If the deal looks like it will produce a good return, they'll point that out and recommend we go after it. The process is nimble because we have a small team and these deals happen fast. An acquisitions person will come to me as soon as they feel confident in their model because they know that timing is critical.

If I want to go through the deals we're considering before a member of the acquisitions team comes to me—perhaps I want to see what's happening—I can look at a pipeline spreadsheet that shows high-level information about the deals. Some of the information in the spreadsheet includes the deal name, the number of units, the year, the return on investment, and so on.

Although we talk throughout the week and have the pipeline spreadsheet so that everyone knows what is going on, we have weekly meetings. Weekly acquisitions meetings or asset management meetings keep us on track. You might think that a small team means that weekly meetings are not necessary; anyone on the team can talk to anyone else whenever they like. However, a weekly meeting for each team enables us to discuss specific issues and become aware of whether we have missed anything. These meetings are fun because we all enjoy looking at the ingredients of the underwriting models. We have similar meetings for the asset management team. It's also fun to review information from the occupancy tracker, which gives an overview of how many leases are in, how many leases are out, how many people visited the leasing office, how many people applied for a lease, and that day's occupancy at each property. The occupancy tracker has built-in metrics that give an idea what the deal is worth today and the projected return, based on various assumptions, if we sold today. At the root of each deal, we're talking about where hardworking people live. It's great to participate in getting people into homes they love. When an apartment complex is 90-plus percent occupied, it's a measure of our success today—the value is net operating income (NOI) driven—as well as our success in the future.

DUNCANVILLE COMMONS OCCUPANCY TRACKER

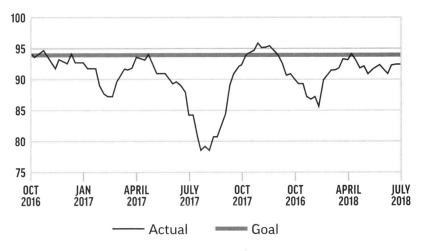

Organizing the Company

To learn about and understand the pros and cons of different organizational structures, I observed how other successful entrepreneurs structure their organizations. I decided, based on success as the main criterion, that to run a good investment firm, I needed the same mind-set as Warren Buffett. His core team is about twenty to thirty employees, but he controls an enormous amount of wealth. I think his success comes from having a very small core team, even though each subsidiary company has many more employees. Likewise, this is the strategy that American Ventures pursued: a small core team of highly talented individuals, and that core team manages anything else.

Throughout this chapter, a key focus has been teaming up to complement strengths and weaknesses in talent and expertise. No one who makes it to the top of an industry does it alone. Even the CEO of a multimillion-dollar company needs mentors. Most companies have a board of directors. This board serves two purposes. One of them is that board members, because of their well-known expertise—their brand—bring credibility to a company. In return for bringing this credibility, many board members receive a fractional percentage of the company's equity.

The other, perhaps more important, purpose is that board members can pitch in their experience to help a CEO and company maneuver through the business process to achieve success. That is, board members provide crucial mentoring to a CEO. Their advice is often not free. At American Ventures, in exchange for bringing on some extremely visible, experienced people as board members, I plan to compensate them from each deal. Everyone wins here. Investors who put between $10 million to $20 million into a deal have confidence in us because of the board members who are advising us. Board members receive fees from a deal or profits at exit. And I get the best mentoring and coaching I can find.

Designing American Ventures around the model of a small core team implies certain things about the organizational structure. At the top is the founder and CEO. Because the company is a commercial real estate investment and operating company, its focus is buying deals. So immediately beneath the CEO and reporting to the CEO is an acquisitions team. The acquisitions team, in addition to a director, has an analyst. Also reporting to the CEO is an asset management team. The acquisitions team coordinates back and forth with the asset management team on every deal we are pursuing. Once we buy a property, the asset management team will take over and run those properties. They work hand in hand with the property management team that oversees day-to-day tasks.

The asset management team also oversees construction management and capital expenditure improvements and renovations. Our focus has always been to invest in value-added deals that require renovating the properties as soon as we acquire them. "Value-added" means that every time you buy an asset, your goal is to create value, so you either build something or modify something that exists. A third possibility is to buy and maintain a well-established property.

Because most deals involve construction or renovation, a good in-house construction manager is essential. Construction management is a personnel-intensive part of the corporation. We typically partner with companies that are extremely good in general contractor work, and our asset management team manages that process. Let's say we buy a property and do a complete face-lift of the exterior, amazing amenities, and interior renovations. Someone has to do all that work, which takes months, and someone has to oversee the process—that's the construction manager. The construction manager hires and manages various contractors or subcontractors who are not the corporation's employees and so are not on the corporation's payroll. The construction manager, who is a corporate employee, manages all the construction projects by delegating to the right people.

A fourth component of the corporate team is property management. The property management team at the site level typically has an apartment complex manager, assistant manager(s), leasing agents, and the maintenance crew.

American Ventures owns and manages many assets. Initially, to prepare for growth, we hired a third-party property management company that was vertically integrated with our team. As we grew, however, we considered owning a subsidiary property management company to do the day-to-day work involved in running an apartment complex. We experimented and acquired one, but later divested it so that we could focus on our core business, which is investments. Once the company grows large enough—say, once it consistently owns 7,000-plus units—we will revisit owning a property management company.

Property management is a specialty in itself. Thus it is most efficient to use the best and brightest property managers already operating in each market and submarket, whether that is Dallas, Austin, or Salt Lake. The cost is upward of 3 percent of a property's revenue, so it makes sense to hire them to do all the groundwork.

A standard set of departments for a large real estate company includes acquisitions, asset management, construction management, and property management. As American Ventures grows, a chief operating officer (COO) will play a pivotal role on the executive team and make the company run smoothly. The COO makes the interweaving functions of these departments run efficiently by ensuring that everyone works together and communicates effectively. You could call a COO the chief facilitator. If someone needs information or a deliverable from another department or is unclear about something, the COO makes sure the lines of communication are open and that information is delivered on time and effectively. The COO makes sure that everyone knows the firm's objectives and their responsibilities and is working toward them.

The following charts show two organizational structures. The first is a traditional hierarchical structure. The second is a more contemporary flat structure.

TRADITIONAL HIERARCHICAL STRUCTURE

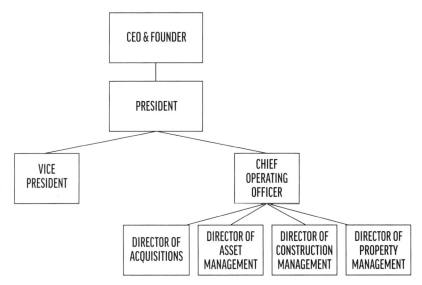

CONTEMPORARY FLAT STRUCTURE

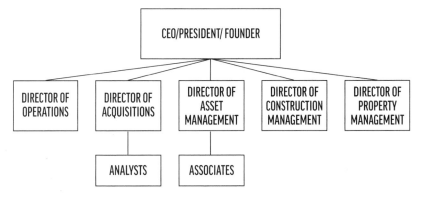

When you start small, as described previously, you can focus your attention on making investment deals and by virtue of that focus steadily grow bigger.

Working with, Not against, Human Nature

In India, we have a proverb: "The drums sound better at a distance." In English, we would say that we tend to like the things we don't have. This is as true in business as anywhere else in life. For example, sometimes when an entrepreneurial venture has co-owners, one owner thinks the other has a more interesting job with extra perks, like attending social events to promote the company. When perceptions about roles diverge like this, it can be difficult to create clear paths about who takes on what duties.

To make co-ownership work, each person needs to feel equally confident that they are benefiting from the relationship. One partner may work in a role that focuses on vision and strategy, raising money, and buying properties, which requires meeting with high-net-worth investors and executives at equity investment firms. In contrast, the other partner may be doing more of the day-to-day operations. Conflict arises when one partner thinks they are doing, say, all the operations work but wants to do at least some of the vision work. Or perhaps the partner doing the vision work wants to explore day-to-day operations but doesn't have those skills. Resolving those conflicts depends on recognizing your and your partner's strengths and weaknesses, talents, and interests, and by being flexible.

Stalemates about what the company should or should not do can develop. When these stalemates do not resolve productively or when the strategic goals are not aligned, one option is to separate. My personal goal always has been to grow the company bigger, sticking to the basics of investment in any real estate cycle, and putting investors' interests above ours. If the market is good when the company sells its assets, then each co-owner realizes a benefit, which is much better than having an unproductive business in which the co-owners are pulling in different directions.

Although most people are ethical and have everyone's interests in mind, some people behave in a more self-interested way. For example, some people will take credit for successes and blame others for failures. Other individuals want to reap the benefits of a reward but don't want to take the risk involved. Comparatively more serious, some individuals are not fair and engage in activities behind a partner's back or take actions to steal ownership of a company. Illegal activities that affect small businesses include fraud and embezzlement. These examples range from individuals breaking the social contract to breaking the law.

Worst-case business scenarios in which individuals harm others—partners, clients, or employees—often make the news. Some high-profile examples include Volkswagen's use of software to falsify the results of emissions tests; Bernie Madoff's use of a Ponzi scheme to embezzle $50 billion from investors; and Enron executives' use of fraudulent accounting practices to embezzle retirement funds from its employees, among other forms of corrupt practices.

THE BEST APPROACH IS TO PUT IN PLACE A LEGAL STRUCTURE THAT PROTECTS YOUR BUSINESS INTERESTS.

One approach to protect yourself from a partner's unethical behavior is to learn enough about a person to determine that they will be a good business partner. The lesson is to take care to do business with people whom you can trust to be working in your best interest and to be honest with you, rather than the opposite. However, cases like Volkswagen, Madoff, and Enron demonstrate that people are not always who they seem to be. Consequently, the best approach is to put in place a legal structure that protects your business interests. Whether this is at big companies like the earlier examples or a small company like ours, the same principles apply.

It All Comes Back to TEAM

A common belief in the early twentieth century was that successful executives worked their way up through the ranks, sometimes starting in the mail room. Without firsthand knowledge of how to make a company's products or deliver its services, an executive would not be able to make good business decisions.

In contrast, twenty-first century business success is about teamwork that produces innovation. The synergy that comes from teamwork lays the foundation for innovation. Teams thrive when people know their roles and perform them excellently. Few companies and business leaders illustrate this better than Starbucks and Howard Schultz.

At the 2018 annual conference of TIGER 21—an investment, personal growth, and philanthropic organization—David Rubenstein, who is cofounder of the private equity firm Carlyle Group and host of *The David Rubenstein Show: Peer-to-Peer Conversations*, and Howard Schultz, former chairman and CEO of Starbucks (he stepped down in 2018), talked together in a panel called "A Tale of Two Titans." Schultz, much admired for his deep belief in doing social good, told the story that when someone asked him if he could make a good coffee, he responded that he didn't think he could make a coffee better than a Starbucks barista. His role, Schultz said, was to build Starbucks into a big company, not to make coffee. To do that, he needed to know a good coffee from a bad coffee and know how to hire people with coffee-making talent or train someone to prepare a good coffee. Schultz and what he achieved at Starbucks illustrate the power of hiring talent to complement your strengths and weaknesses. Starbucks also illustrates the power of teamwork. Together, Schultz and Starbucks baristas created a multibillion-dollar company from a single coffee shop in Seattle.

EXECUTIVE SUMMARY

- Identify your strengths and weaknesses. Analyze your weaknesses to identify any that you can effectively strengthen. Then locate a skillful and trusted partner or mentor who can teach you how to boost your performance in those weak areas.

- When making decisions about your team, maintain your goal of creating a win-win situation for the team, the company board of directors, the founder or owner, and the investors. Knowing and balancing all stakeholders' interests is critical.

- Understand that talent is a combination of natural ability in an area, interest, and the willingness to let interest drive you to pursue excellence.

- To know what kind of team you want and need, understand your strengths and weaknesses.

- Devote time to finding, hiring, and incentivizing people with talent and experience to avoid the unacceptably high cost of a lack of experience.

- Find and work with a mentor, or more than one, whose strengths complement your weaknesses.

- Offer a percentage of commercial real estate deals as a return for hard work.

- Publicly show you value your team and the drive to excel. Build a close-knit team by celebrating success and communicating with transparency.

- Structure your organization to enable the CEO and directors to do their best work.

CHAPTER 4

USING TIME AND LEVERAGE TO SEIZE OPPORTUNITY

n the months leading up to the 2008 financial crisis, I noticed a lot of activity in the subprime loan segment of the lending industry. I sold four or five homes from my portfolio to people who wanted to buy and were using subprime, no-documentation loans, but I always wondered what would happen if they missed one payment. I began to sense a market correction coming because of the way banks were making loans. For example, an airport mechanic who worked for Boeing—so he had a good job—bought five homes from me without sending documentation to the bank. It was as if the loan officer said, "He's a flight mechanic, so he could be making $150,000." These are called stated income loans. The lender literally takes the buyer's word for it. All they do is pull a credit report. These no-documentation loans were happening to such an extent that I thought it was too good to be true and would not sustain.

In 2007, the financial industry was violating the 101 of lending practice: don't lend to people who can't pay back. Banks were making large loans to people who would not be able to pay them back. It was a systemic issue that started with the biggest of the big banks and financial institutions and went all the way down to the smallest of the small lenders.

Most of the homes I invested in were in the median price range, $150,000 to $200,000, in San Antonio. A few were in the $300,000 to $500,000, which was a lot for a home in San Antonio ten years ago. While median homes are great rental homes, expensive homes are not. Experience told me that if there was any kind of market correction, those big homes would be a problem. If my tenants had any issue, like a big medical bill, they would miss a payment.

Another signal that a correction was coming was information I saw from a title attorney I know. He was closing deals left and right, most of them no-documentation, subprime loans. Again, it was too good to be true. All these bits of information piled up and told me the boom was too good. Putting these factors together, I knew my big homes would be my biggest liability if no one was living there or if I could not sell them at the same price or more than what I bought them for. So I started selling them. Months later, the biggest financial crisis in my lifetime happened.

I LISTENED TO THESE SIGNALS, SAW THE CONSEQUENCES COMING, AND MADE A COURSE CORRECTION.

I was right to trust my gut. But understanding what was going on was more than intuition. My background in science, in part, enabled me to notice these factors at the right time and put together the picture of what was happening. I listened to these signals, saw the consequences coming, and made a course correction. When everyone else was floundering in the financial meltdown that followed, I was repositioning and planning my next steps.

Postcorrection, I focused on another big principle, economies of scale: advancing from single-family investments to multifamily investments, apart from other commercial real estate investments or opportunistic residential investments.

When most people think about real estate investing, they think of wheeling and dealing with lots of drama. But you can take a systematic approach that balances risk and opportunity, cash and leverage, and careful research.

This story boils down to a few key principles. Know your industry by doing the research. Be systematic in using this information. Pay close attention to timing. Understand the downsides before they are likely to happen.

Effectively using prep time to work with these key principles is how you pull together a successful commercial real estate deal. Prep time is what enables you to take advantage of timing and strike a balance between cash and loan in your capital stack. And your reputation is essential to closing the deals.

There are three factors in successfully executing a real estate deal: finding the right property, finding the property at the right time, and setting the deal in motion at the right time. Doing the right thing at the right time is essential for the deal, and prep time is critical to achieving this timing.

The Pipeline:
Finding the Right Property

Finding the right properties is an ongoing process. We are constantly looking for and reviewing deals. It is not as if one day we say, "Hey, you know what? Let's do deals analysis this week." We keep track of potential deals in a document called a pipeline spreadsheet, and we are always adding potential deals to it.

We continuously review deals in the pipeline. You can spend hours and hours on a deal that may not be the right deal to invest in, so you must do a quick, high-level analysis and create a short list to analyze further. We may start with a list of fifty to one hundred potential deals in the pipeline and focus on what we think are the three, four, or five best deals to pursue. For those three to five deals, we request information from either the owner or a broker; we sign a confidentiality agreement to get this information. The information includes rent rolls, operating income statements—everything we need to create a financial underwriting model.

Once we get enough information, we use it to develop assumptions that form the basis of the underwriting model for the deal. First, we assume a value for the purchase price. Then we lay out a business plan: do we want to buy the property, stabilize it, refinance, pull out some cash, and hold onto it for the long-term? Or do we want to hold it short-term and sell for a profit? How does each plan fit with other investments we have, for example, other investments that we bought and hold for the cash flow? When we evaluate a potential deal, we always look for what's called value-add, where we buy and invest an amount of money into the deal so that we can create value. Our goal is to drive gross rental revenue up, bring operating expenses down, and increase the net operating income (NOI).

Due Diligence:
Is It Really the Property We Think It Is?

Notice that we assume many things to build the underwriting model. An underwriting model is only as good as its assumptions. And if you can support assumptions with reality, the underwriting model will be stronger. The most important thing to do during prep time is the due diligence property visits that go into determining whether a deal is even a good idea—testing the underwriting model's assumptions against reality.

Let's say we look at a property with a purchase price of $10 million. We perform extensive due diligence, starting with touring the property—this helps us ascertain the visual condition of the property, beyond all the fancy pictures we see in brokers' or owners' packages. In addition, we take contractors to evaluate a property. The tour and contractor evaluation tell us whether we can create value and how much money we will have to put into a deal to create that value. Suppose when you look at the property, you see that things are falling apart outside: it has broken siding in places, the paint is chipped, the walkways are uneven, the clubhouse is in disrepair, the pool is old. We also tour several comparable properties in the neighborhood and prepare a good market survey, in addition to gathering information from data tools like CoStar. (See chapter 2.) Based on what we see, we start putting together a renovation budget. The $10 million purchase price, renovation budget, and other closing costs help you come up with the total deal cost.

To make any deal profitable, we need to borrow a low-interest debt. Let's say we put together a deal that includes the $10 million purchase price plus $2 million to renovate the property, called capital expenditure (capex). The total cost basis is $12 million. We typically approach Fannie Mae– and Freddie Mac–backed lenders to obtain 65–70 percent loan-to-cost loans.

We became very good at executing these value-add deals. We spend time improving the exterior, the leasing office, the clubhouse, the pool and deck, and other amenities. We create beautiful common areas because they give people pride of ownership. Most of our deals are workforce housing; giving people a feeling of pride when they walk in improves our percentage of units rented. We also renovate the interiors—improve the flooring, the countertops and backsplashes, and light fixtures; use trendy two-tone paint; and so on—and then we charge a premium for those units, comparable to the market.

We look at the state of other properties in the area—the surrounding area defines a property's market. This is another important factor of due diligence. Being the first in the market to renovate a property entails taking a risk because you might not be able to raise rents aggressively without data to back the increase. It is equally risky to be the last to renovate, because, again, the ability to raise rents will be uncertain. When we buy in the middle phase of renovations in a market, the risk is minimal, and the return is high. For example, let's say there are ten properties in the immediate submarket—four of them have been renovated, and the renovated unit rents are higher. We want to implement the same or a similar program; in the majority of cases, we don't need to do better or reinvent the wheel. During our due diligence phase, we assess the state of the market and what degree of renovation will be needed. Before we make a deal and prepare a contract, we spend a lot of time going to the properties and touring the assets.

The first step in any dealmaking is sending a letter of intent, or LOI, to a potential seller or the broker who is marketing the property. Although you make an offer, you have the option to back out of a deal between the letter of intent and the purchase contract. Our intent all the time is to close a deal but perform substantial due diligence to determine that the offer we submit really is viable. One reason we win a lot of deals is that we put in a good amount of work to evaluate the property before signing a purchase contract. Once we offer a letter of intent, we don't revise or rescind the offer; we go to the actual purchase and sale agreement. Consequently, we have demonstrated to sellers in general that if they put together a deal with us, we are very serious about closing—this is our reputation, our brand. Unless a seller docsn't perform on their side of a contract, we strive to close every deal we put under contract. Our due diligence process enables us to use this approach.

We benefit from devoting prep time to due diligence in two other ways. First, our underwriting models are low risk because due diligence enables us to have confidence in our assumptions. While we are conducting due diligence, we are finding the best financing for the deal. Again, this enables us to create a very sound underwriting model. Second, when we have term sheets from the lenders and then approach sellers, they know we are serious.

Given what we do during prep time, you might think it takes us months to put together a deal. But when we identify a "best" opportunity, we need to move fast. Sometimes, we have only a few days for prep. For example, an owner might be in distress for some reason and willing to sell immediately to the first reasonable buyer. Most of the time, the seller wants to make sure that the fact a property is being sold does not disrupt operations. The moment staff know that the seller is selling the property, they worry that they will be out a job; in that case, property operations may decrease in quality, and the value of the property will likewise decrease. When we are considering a deal, we must respect the impact on the seller's asset. A third reason we move fast is to create the deal before there is competition for it; competition drives up the price. We strive to win off-market deals directly from the seller or preempt the deal with a broker with a first look before they take it to the wider market or engage in fully marketing the property.

To avoid alarming staff, sometimes we do a property visit as if we plan to rent an apartment. We do the same thing when we visit neighboring properties. Other times we say that we are looking to invest in the area and are doing some comparable research. And still other times, with prior authorization from the seller, we say that we are inspecting the property for appraisal, for insurance purposes, or on behalf of the lender. The approach we use depends on the individual deal and the need to respect sellers' confidentiality requests. For example, if a deal is fully marketed with a broker, the whole world knows the property is for sale. This situation is straightforward. We set up an appointment and do the tour. At the opposite extreme is an off-market deal. In this case, the seller does not want his or her operations staff to know the property is being sold, and we need to use a kind of mystery shopping approach.

We regularly look at the properties in the pipeline to see which deals are active or dead. We'll investigate anything that's active. We begin by interacting with the seller or broker. In the next step, before we visit the property, we improvise an underwriting model with lots of broad assumptions. Then we tour the property and fine-tune our assumptions.

We visit the surrounding area and comparable properties and refine our assumptions about the market. We look at the community. Are the cars mostly old? Do the surrounding properties look appealing or do they have litter or junk in public areas? We make a good guess about whether people living in the surrounding neighborhoods are in the workforce; we care about who lives in the neighborhood because we focus on workforce housing. If the neighborhood is mostly workforce housing and the cars in parking lots look taken care of, then we infer that the property location is a stable neighborhood. On the other hand, if people are loitering on the streets, we infer that the neighborhood is rough, which has a negative impact on the property's value.

At this point, if a deal looks good enough, we visit the property and walk around to see what the opportunity is. If the management company is good and has decent revenue, they'll keep up the property. If not, you'll see signs that a management company is not maintaining a property: the landscaping is not kept up, or mud is everywhere because there are no rainwater drains or they are not properly maintained, and so on. These downsides might be part of the opportunity because they are simple to fix. My ideal is typically a deal that's broken, mismanaged, with an out-of-town, out-of-state, or out-of-country owner, off market, and in a good location or in the path of regentrification. When all these factors align in a deal, we call it a "perfect storm."

We also take a contractor who can look deeper; for example, the contractor will check the foundations and the roof, which need more thorough inspection. Upon execution of a purchase and sale agreement (PSA), we get professional third-party reports, which typically include a property condition assessment report (PCA), commonly called a property condition report (which is like a residential home inspection report), a zoning report, and a phase 1 environmental site assessment (ESA) report. Lenders require these reports before they will finance a deal. An outlier story in chapter 5 demonstrates why these detailed reports are critical in their own right, aside from lender requirements.

While we have been conducting site visits, we also have been evaluating lenders and finding the right loan for the deal. Is the correct loan source Fannie Mae or Freddie Mac? Should we get a bridge loan? Should we get a floating-rate loan or a fixed-rate loan, which means we will have long-term debt? The answer to this question depends on the business model we choose. If we plan to hold the property for five to seven years, or even longer, then a low-interest, fixed-rate loan is the better choice; if the plan is to hold on to the deal for a shorter term, such as three to five years, then a bridge loan or floating-rate Fannie or Freddie loan—the interest rate adjusts with the market—is the better choice. We decide who our investment partners will be, how much equity to put into the deal, and establish the capital stack. All this information goes into the underwriting model.

With this fine-tuned model, if the deal looks like an opportunity, we submit a letter of intent. We will use what we learned from the site visit to justify our offer if the seller has a higher asking price; for example, we'll list property flaws, like a roof that needs to be replaced or cracks in the foundation, with an estimate of what it costs to fix them. The seller knows every flaw and will make every effort to close the deal in the shortest time.

Using Prep Time to Find Off-Market Deals

One valuable thing you can do during prep time is keep in touch with industry colleagues. For example, off-market deals don't make it into the pipeline because they are off market. We learn about off-market deals from prior relationships. For example, I may talk with an owner over the years and learn they are planning to retire and move on. Or maybe an owner tells me they are in some kind of distress. My team has long-term relationships as well; each member of my organization has ten to thirty years of experience in the industry. In Dallas we found one of the biggest deals we ever invested in, a portfolio of eight properties, because of a prior relationship with the owner, with whom we kept in contact over the years; when he turned eighty, he decided to sell and move on. We bought this deal directly from him. Other deals come from insurance brokers or contractors. When you spend time maintaining your relationships with people, you make good use of prep time.

In commercial real estate, the amount of prep time you devote to setting up a deal must be flexible. Without flexibility, you cannot be in the right place at the right time to execute a deal. Having a pipeline of deals enables us to exercise this flexibility.

Setting Things in Motion with the Right Elements in Place

To execute the best deals, you must set things in motion at the right time with the right elements in place. Prep time and your pipeline help you identify and confirm the best deals. But without the right timing and the right elements, it's unlikely a deal will happen.

Knowing what the right time is—and, possibly, how to determine the right time—may be partly a matter of intuition built on experience. But there is an identifiable window of opportunity. It is better to be the first to bid on a property so that you don't have competition. Competitors for a deal will drive up the price. They will also create challenges that you might not foresee.

In early 2015, we were expanding our portfolio in two major markets of Texas: Dallas–Fort Worth and Houston. Both cities were among the top-ranked US multifamily investment markets for several years. I believe strongly in economies of scale in the value-add space, especially having acquired a 327-unit deal in San Antonio, and I was going after bigger assets or a portfolio of assets in 2015. Typically, on these deals, the market sets the price; there is no set sales price.

We identified an 848-unit deal in the Houston energy corridor and made it into the seller's top two potential buyers. When the seller interviewed us, he liked our underwriting model, capex budget, operating budget, the due diligence work we did, and our future business plan. The seller even agreed to meet with us in our Austin office. After our presentation, the seller told us that we were the best buyer for the deal. We did not win the offer.

YOU LEARN MORE FROM YOUR FAILURES THAN SUCCESSES.

Why? Even though we were fully capable of buying the asset, the other competitive offer had equity capital ready to deploy. Our proven track record was not enough to close the deal; to close the deal, we needed to have an equity partner lined up. The experience taught me a lot. You learn more from your failures than successes.

A few months later, another opportunity came along. In hindsight, 2015 was one of the hottest years to acquire deals in the Dallas–Fort Worth metropolitan statistical area. This deal was being fully marketed by a top brokerage firm in the Dallas market. The seller was a national player, Carlyle, and it was a 650-unit deal—exactly the size deal we were looking for. The deal passed all our underwriting guidelines, and we narrowed down the price to match the pricing guidance. Once again, we were extremely effective in the buyer interview process. We impressed the seller that we meant business and had the capability and debt and equity capital necessary to close the deal. During the interview process, we shared our track record and our equity partners' track record. We also confidentially shared our and our equity partners' balance sheets to show that we had the necessary funds to close the deal. This time, we seized the opportunity when it presented itself.

Experience taught us that knowing our weaknesses was as

important as knowing our strengths. Our weaknesses included that we were not as big a firm as our competing bidders, didn't have a track record of owning and operating a deal as big as the one we were trying to acquire, and, most important, did not have committed equity partners. In contrast, our strengths included having a proven track record of closing deals on time and having closed 100 percent of the deals we put under contract. To overcome our chief weakness, we aligned ourselves with an equity partner and did a joint-venture deal. Our equity partner owned and operated several billion dollars of deals and had the balance sheet to deploy the equity capital. When I submitted the letter of intent, we demonstrated the strengths of our combined team. This time we won the deal.

Balancing Cash and Borrowing

An underwriting model is, at heart, a risk analysis. That risk analysis is essential for understanding how much of your own money to put into a deal and how much to borrow. The lender also has an underwriting model. The key indicator they use to determine the risk of a deal is the debt-service coverage ratio (DSCR). When your risk analysis and the lender's risk analysis are close, then you can put a deal together.

Let's say, for example, the total cost of a deal is $15 million. You can borrow 65, 70, or 75 percent of the cost depending on your DSCR. Ideally, to have good returns, you want to put more loan into the deal and less equity. But what is the balance point, and how do you know when you've struck the right balance?

When a deal generates enough net operating income—the revenue is enough to support the debt and the expenses, and still generate cash flow—we can go for higher leverage. This balance depends on the market. Change in occupancy is the main factor driving cash flow. For example, in a Dallas–Fort Worth area deal, the chance of a 95 percent occupancy property dropping to 85 percent is low. A 10 percent drop in occupancy would significantly reduce a property's cash flow. In this market, we can be aggressive and borrow 70 or even 75 percent of the funds for the deal because the property, in the current market, can easily support the loan, pay all the expenses, and still generate cash flow.

Real estate deals are trickier in tertiary markets. Take Killeen, Texas: the local economy there depends on the Fort Hood military base, which is among the largest military bases in the world. About 35,000 military personnel are assigned to Fort Hood, but deployments occur often. The population of Killeen is about 145,000, so the military presence is about 25 percent of the local population. When a military deployment occurs, it is possible for a property's occupancy to go from 90 percent to 80 percent overnight.

UNDERSTANDING THE DYNAMICS OF THE PRIMARY, SECONDARY, AND TERTIARY MARKETS ENABLES YOU TO STRIKE THE RIGHT BALANCE BETWEEN CASH AND BORROWING.

Commercial real estate deals must take into account that a property's cash flow can change radically in a short time. Because we are aware of the impact of rapid occupancy changes, we structure the amount of loan versus equity for a deal in Killeen differently than we structure a deal in primary markets like Dallas–Fort Worth. Understanding the dynamics of the primary, secondary, and tertiary markets enables you to strike the right balance between cash and borrowing.

Leveraging Timing as the Best Strategy for a Deal

The basic wisdom in investing, whether it's the stock market or commercial real estate, is to create a gap between the buying price and the selling price—in other words, buy low and sell high. The underwriting model spells out what the minimum acceptable gap is, based on the KPI of 20 percent IRR. The question, of course, is how do you know when prices are low and when the market is at a peak? In real time, you make only educated guesses. Make no mistake: timing is the critical element.

For business reasons unrelated to the state of the market, in 2018 we were careful about buying properties. Our midrange plan was to sell properties sometime between 2018 and 2020. Did we know what part of the market cycle we were in—the middle to late part of the cycle? No. However, in the first three-quarters of 2018, all market conditions said we were at or near a peak, so we decided to sell earlier than planned. We sold for higher prices than we were expecting and made higher returns. Those higher prices told us we were taking the right approach.

To get higher returns than expected requires a combination of factors to align. First, you need to have a plan to sell, whether short-range like two to three years or midrange like three to five years. This plan sets up the timing. Second, you need to be flexible: content to wait or happy to move quickly. Third, you need to stay informed about the state of the market. The state of the market is what should trigger you to execute your plan quickly, say over a six-month period.

Staying informed about the state of the market is critical. With constant vigilance, sometimes circumstances happen that may help you for the better. Being prepared to benefit from the circumstances requires flexibility as well as vigilance.

Taking a flexible approach depends on the condition of the property. When its condition is less than top-notch—that is, you did not invest in the property—you cannot take advantage of the market at its peak. This is not a situation where you can scramble to fix a property. You cannot improve your occupancy rate overnight. Even though you can improve the grounds in a couple of days, you cannot do the same for units or amenities—the pool, the clubhouse, exercise facilities, the parking lot—that do not meet the local market standard. If you don't continually maintain your property, you may have to sell at a lower price than what you would like.

Another factor that affects the ability to take advantage of circumstances is the kind of loan funding the deal. How long you planned at the outset to hold on to a property influences what kind of a loan—fixed rate or floating rate—you can get. The type of loan and when you sell a property together create opportunities and issues. Generally, a fixed-rate loan means that market rates no longer play a role in decisions, but it comes with a hefty prepayment penalty, whereas a floating-rate loan means you need to watch market rates very closely but gives flexibility to pay off the loan, mostly without a prepayment penalty past one year.

For example, in 2015 we bought a property in Dallas for $34 million. The partner in this deal was a big family office. Looking toward the future from the vantage point of 2015, we planned to hold this asset for three to five years at least. We believed that between 2015 and 2020, the interest rates would go up, so we went for a fixed-rate loan. A fixed-rate loan provides a very good interest rate, but the financial institution wants to lock in the loan for ten years.

If you bought a deal with a fixed-rate loan for ten years but decide to sell in three to five years, you must pay a massive prepayment penalty, generally called yield maintenance, for paying off the loan early. On a $34 million deal, that penalty can be as high as $3.5 to $4 million. It usually runs from about 7 to 10 percent of the loan, dependent on the ten-year Treasury rate. Whether yield maintenance is at the low end or the high end depends on how much time on the loan is left. That's a lot of money to pay if you sell a property sooner than you planned, let's say in three or four years.

There is a way to offset this damaging situation. We can sell the property and the buyer assumes the loan. Essentially, we sell both the property and the loan. To make the deal even better, the buyer can get a supplemental loan up to 75 percent of the new value at the current loan rate. So the buyer gets our loan, which has an interest rate lower than the current market rate, and borrows as much as 75 percent of the new value through a supplemental loan at the current market rates to cover the difference between the original loan amount and the new purchase price. On top of that, the first buyer can in turn sell the property to a second buyer with the same loan assumption. A property can swap owners twice on one low-interest rate loan under current Fannie Mae guidelines.

When we plan three to five years into the future, loan assumption gives us flexibility. Lenders base the interest rate they charge on a market spread over the ten-year Treasury rate; in mid-2019, the ten-year Treasury rate was 2.32. So we can buy a property at approximately a 4.5 percent interest rate, which will be locked in at that fixed rate until the loan maturity date. Most multifamily loans at the time of origination come with the flexibility of making interest-only payments for two to three years and longer. Interest-only payments keep our monthly loan payments lower since we are only paying for the interest, not the principal; this is especially useful during the value-add phase.

In 2018, we sold the assets that we bought in 2015. With our effective acquisition process, efficient operations, and better market conditions, the values of our assets went up substantially. But interest rates remained low. In these market conditions, it was relatively easy to find a buyer willing to pay a premium for the property. But rather than assume an existing loan, the buyer wanted to get a new loan to take advantage of the two- to three-year interest-only payments that come with new loans. At that point, our net proceeds from the sale were less by the amount equal to the prepayment penalty. We still made a good profit from the sale. However, it prompted us to evaluate floating-rate loans, which have no prepayment penalties, on future acquisitions.

With market conditions remaining good, if a buyer wants to get a new loan, we have the option of selling deals for a higher price so we can offset some of the prepayment penalty. Buyers, in turn, have an option of paying a lower price if they want to assume the loan. Markets are dynamic, and, most of the time, this gives us many options—that's the beauty of capitalism. 2018 was one of my most profitable years in CRE investing.

In 2016 and after, our strategic plan called for short-term deals. Interest rates had been steady for the past year or so, and we planned to hold the properties for only two to three years, so we acquired most of the deals with Fannie Mae floating-rate loans. Since they were short-term deals, there was no reason to get a ten-year fixed-rate loan. Based on those experiences, we changed plans for the next year because interest rates didn't go up much. Most of the floating-rate loans were based on the London Interbank Offered Rate (LIBOR); the LIBOR is an index based on the average interest rate at which international banks loan funds to each other in London. A thirty-year LIBOR chart shows periods of extreme volatility. To offset this volatility and cover our basis, whenever we get floating-rate loans, we also buy an interest rate cap for LIBOR. The interest rate cap pays us funds when the LIBOR exceeds a certain percentage, and these funds cover the additional payment when the interest rate rises.

Commercial real estate deals depend on local markets and on what is happening in the national economy. In 2018, because of liquidity in the market, better bridge loans were also available. Bridge loans typically are not fixed-rate loans; the interest rate floats based on a benchmark index like LIBOR. Fannie Mae and Freddie Mac loans have fixed and floating rates. The interest rates on fixed-rate loans are based on Treasury rates, while floating-rate loans are pegged to the LIBOR. To choose between the different types of loans, you must watch how the Treasury rates and LIBOR change. In 2018, Treasury rates went up because the Fed raised interest rates to marginally reduce the attractiveness of borrowing and, in turn, help combat asset inflation from a heated market; the interest rate on floating-rate loans fluctuated with LIBOR. Our analysts monitor these rates, but no one can tell what will happen with interest rates six months in the future. To account for this uncertainty, we always stress test a deal's underwriting model assuming that rates are going up by at least half a point to one point every year. Since rates remained pretty consistent in recent years, we beat our cash flow projections.

An Opportunistic Deal, or Your Reputation Is the Thing

Commercial real estate has at least two different classes of assets: property and land. So far, we've been talking about property assets, like apartment complexes. We also talked about residential real estate, which is where I started. After working in single-family investments in Texas for a few years, I was ready to do the next big thing. I would come to learn that land deals offered some interesting possibilities.

I moved to Austin and looked at what else I could do. Austin was—and still is—regentrifying on its east side, so I researched that area. At the time, I was a solo operation with a few consultants and worked out of a coworking space in downtown Austin. Because I worked out of this coworking space, I met President Obama, who came to visit this emerging epicenter and incubator of tech start-ups. At coworking spaces, you get to hang out with some amazing entrepreneurs, mostly in technology, but everyone has something on the side in real estate. And the watercooler and hallway conversations are incredible. Almost as good as meeting President Obama, I heard a Formula 1 racetrack was coming to Austin.

The United States Grand Prix was coming to Austin—it was a $200 million flex investment—and that grabbed my attention. At first, I thought Formula 1 was not going to work in Austin; this is mainly a place for music. SXSW, Austin City Limits—there is a music festival in Austin every month of the year. Besides music, Austin has the University of Texas Longhorns Big 12 football team. My second thought was that the city was not at all ready for a racetrack. At the same time, I knew the Grand Prix was going to be big because Formula 1 is big elsewhere in the world. It's a big brand with an international and domestic audience, a combination with the means and capability to survive. The idea of an international audience set me thinking.

I learned that the project was real, not just watercooler gossip—but it was behind schedule. The plan was to open the track on August 20, 2012. But in early July, forty days before the opening date, they were still digging. At that point, I became curious about who was involved in the project. I knew that Red McCombs, an eighty-something billionaire from San Antonio, was involved; the University of Texas at Austin School of Business is named after him. At the time, I thought McCombs was building his legacy and wouldn't do anything likely to fail. I believed the other investors involved would do everything in their power to make it successful as well. I had visions of big, international-quality hotel complexes.

So I decided to piggyback on their bet and looked for land in that area. No one was selling. And then I found it. I heard about a seller in distress who wanted to sell his home and move on. When I contacted the broker, I learned that another person was looking at the property, had signed a contract, but was still negotiating. I stepped in and said, "I'll close the deal in ten days. No loan. I'm going to pay cash. I'll send the earnest money this second." The broker immediately drafted a purchase and sale agreement, ran to an escrow company, and deposited the money—all while the other buyer was still negotiating a lower price.

Although I had cash immediately available for earnest money, I did not have the full purchase price. I went to a bank where I had a line of credit, but they said it would take fifteen to twenty days to get an appraisal. The bank didn't think we could close the deal in ten days. I said, "No, I need to close the deal. This is an amazing deal. I already have a guidance line of credit." In a guidance line of credit, the bank prequalifies you for a line of credit up to a certain amount, but it requires that the lender vet the property, rather than your creditworthiness. They might have $1 million to transfer to you immediately, but they want to make sure you're putting the money into the right deal. And for the bank, that means getting a written, approved, and signed appraisal of the property's value. The bank researched the deal, talked with their CEO, and immediately sent an appraiser to the property. The appraiser saw what I saw: the property was worth a lot more than the purchase price. The bank released the money on a verbal appraisal while the actual written appraisal was on its way, and I closed the deal. This is the power of relationship.

I ended up leaving that land alone for a long time. The property was on the east side of Austin, and the US Grand Prix and Formula 1 racetrack was a success. So I used the land for parking. It generated money so I could pay the taxes and maintain the land. The land value almost tripled between 2012 when I bought and today.

Recently, with the new 2017 tax reforms and qualified opportunity zones in place, we learned that the land I purchased prior to the inaugural US Grand Prix race is in an opportunity zone. With preferential tax treatment from the opportunity zone—capital gains from investing in an opportunity zone are tax free, provided you hold the investment for ten years—businesses have an incentive for long-term investment in the area. Now, my land, apart from being in the opportunity zone, is also in the path of regentrification. It realized the value much more than what I spotted years ago. We're hiring engineers to perform a site assessment, the beginning of a long approval process, so we can build an apartment complex.

Time enabled me to realize the value in this land. But the deal made me look beyond buying multifamily residential properties. Today, I focus on workforce housing, but I wonder about opportunities I am missing. This is basic economics. Every choice you make has an opportunity cost. If I make this deal, what opportunity of equal value am I not choosing? If I stay in real estate, what opportunities do I forgo? Consider ultrasuccessful individuals, like Jeff Bezos, Bill Gates, and Warren Buffett. By virtue of their focus in other industries, particularly technology, they created an exponential growth path. I envision doing the same, thinking about multifamily residential deals as my anchor and looking into other areas. For example, what other ways can I create value in opportunity zones?

Some of my thoughts are about diversification as well. There is a huge opportunity in senior housing. Baby boomers are retiring—we're in the middle of that arc—with ten thousand people in the United States turning sixty every day. At the beginning of my real estate career, I innovated in a way that helped people with poor credit histories become successful homeowners. Now I wonder: Can I innovate to help seniors with their housing needs? I'll talk more about these opportunities in chapter 8, which focuses on the future.

EXECUTIVE SUMMARY

- Remember the three factors to successful execution of a real estate deal: finding the right property, finding the property at the right time, and setting the deal in motion at the right time.

- Use prep time to build a pipeline of properties that meet your investment criteria.

- Gather enough detailed information on three to five of the best properties in the pipeline to build a rough underwriting model and business plan for each.

- Use due diligence procedures, including evaluating lenders, to test the underwriting model's assumptions.

- During prep time, keep in touch with colleagues to be the first to find a good off-market deal.

- Once you determine the right timing, ensure you have the right elements in place—for example, an equity partner in addition to financing—to demonstrate to the buyer that you can close the deal.

- Consider your investors as part of your team.

- Know the characteristics of the asset you plan to acquire and the market it is in so that you can strike the best balance between equity and loan.

- Stay informed about the state of the market, and create and execute business plans with built-in flexible timing to sell at or near the market peak.

- Understand how your business plan and the type of loan you have—fixed or floating—interact with market forces to create opportunities or risks.

- When you go into opportunistic deals, don't be afraid to hold the asset until the right development opportunity becomes available. That is, think about how you can leverage time to create value.

CHAPTER 5

THE POTENTIAL OF DOWNSIDES

D ownsides can delay a deal, elevate risks, or do both. Because they relate to risk, downsides sound like threats. What's the difference? With a downside, if you find ways to course correct, there's a way to lift the downside into positive territory. A threat is more fundamental. If you don't see it in advance, it may be too late to do a course correction when you do see it. For example, we were at risk of losing part of the principal on a deal. Out of thousands of units we owned, this risk developed on only one deal. When you lose principal, you lose part of the investment you put into the deal—you never want to lose principal. That was a threat we didn't see in advance.

Sam Zell, at a TIGER 21 annual meeting, said sometimes we have to cut losses and move on. However, I always make time to reflect before moving on because the failures taught me more than all the good investments we made over the years. This chapter is about what those one or two failed deals taught me.

Identifying Downsides and Problems before They Are Likely to Happen

There is a gray area between downsides and threats because timing—in advance or too late—is critical. The essential difference is that you notice a downside when you still have time to do something about it. You are more at the mercy of a threat. From that perspective, there is a continuum between threats, downsides, and upsides.

For example, we know that B and C properties—workforce multifamily residences in nice locations with rents that average-income people can afford, but that have not been kept up—do well in markets that are in the path of gentrification. When we buy the property, we renovate the interior by putting in nicer two-tone paint, appliances, countertops, fixtures, and flooring—these are not expensive upgrades—and we do an amazing exterior lift. Because we do these renovations, the upsell is substantial, and the property may become a C to B-minus or B-minus to a B asset.

A potential downside is whether we are the first in the area to upgrade a property. If so, we are taking a bigger risk than if we were in the middle of the pack. If we are the first, then we can't tell whether renovation is going to yield a return on the investment. However, if comparable properties have done similar upgrades—that is, you are in the middle of the pack—you can evaluate whether upgrading your property is worth the expense. With the proper research, we can do a course correction. Doing the research to evaluate whether you are in the middle of a neighborhood renovation offsets the risk.

In contrast, let's say we have a C-minus property that we think is in the path of gentrification. As part of research on the property, we carefully investigate the area, look into trends from the past few years, and occasionally speak with the city manager to find out if the city has any specific plans for that neighborhood in the coming years. Suppose the city manager says the city is putting more money into the area. Also suppose that three blocks on either side of the property are well into the gentrification process. This information would lead us to think it was only a matter of time before the two blocks surrounding the target property would be gentrified. Based on these assumptions, we would think the property could become a solid C value-added deal, so we would pursue it. After buying the property, we would implement the value-added plan by renovating with upgrades. If the assumptions that the deal rests on do not come to pass—the path of gentrification misses the property site, the city doesn't put money into the area, and so on—the property will not produce the rent or occupancy that would justify the renovation.

The threat—not a downside—in a situation like this would be that you are wrong. If an area has been distressed for a long time and the path of gentrification missed it, you would not be able to justify an investment in renovation. It wouldn't matter if you put in gold-plated light fixtures, or any fixtures, because no one would pay higher rent in that neighborhood. If the path of gentrification misses a neighborhood, you can't charge higher rent that would offset renovation expenses. In this case, you may have to cut your losses and move on. You can't retenant the property with a better tenant profile while you are holding the asset if the area is not improving.

Moving on in real estate is not a complete loss, like it might be in other industries. In real estate, there's always a way to recoup most of the cost because property is a tangible asset. You might lose some money, but you don't lose entirely. A $9 million property will sell for $7 million or $8 million; the sale price is not zero.

It does not make sense to look into a D property unless someone is selling a $10 million property for $6 million. In that case, the possibility of making modest renovations in line with the neighborhood is built into the deal because there is a $4 million gap between the valuation and the sale price. When the location is distressed, it doesn't work to buy a property with a $10 million value for $11 million and try to make it into a $15 million property. That's the threat you must catch. There is no way to turn the downside of a distressed location into a positive.

In some cases, being the first to do something can be to your advantage. One C class property of ours had security gates when most of the neighborhood properties had no gated entry—but they were not working. We upgraded them, put in security cameras, and eventually hired a security guard for the property. The cost added $60,000 to $80,000 a year to the expenses. We financed the property through a Fannie Mae loan, and to obtain a good leveraged loan, Fannie Mae underwriters insisted that we install security cameras. The total security upgrade added $150,000 maximum to expenses, but along with our other renovations, it gave a boost of $2 to $3 million on the bottom line. The impact on the bottom line was this large because tenants benefited directly from the improved security system. In this case, we identified a downside to the property itself, remedied it, and turned it into an upside.

Stress Testing the Underwriting Model: A Primary Defense against Downsides and Threats

In some cases, the opportunity in a deal may not unfold as planned. Generally, we hold on to a property for cash flow and sell for a profit in three to five years. We usually make the decision about how long to hold a property during our underwriting process. However, if the cash flow or sale price we anticipated doesn't come through, we may have to change plans.

Initially, when we decide on the time line for a property, we stress test the underwriting model to evaluate how robust it is. The key question is whether the underwriting model is sufficiently resilient if we do not get the returns that we are looking for in the anticipated time frame. Recall (from chapter 2) that stress testing involves changing basic inputs in the underwriting model, like net operating income (NOI), interest rates, costs, rent, or other variables, and evaluating the impact on key performance indicators and the internal rate of return. Suppose the initial plan is to hold a property for three to five years. During stress testing, we look at what could happen if we hold it for seven to ten years. We hope that, even with extra scrutiny, if we hold the property for seven to ten years instead of selling it in three to five years, the chances of getting the kind of return we're looking for is high. When we hold a property for seven to ten years, we assess whether we get the same internal rate of return or multiple. At the other end of the spectrum, if we are conservative and underwrite the deal with potential higher interest rate increases during the hold time or lower rent increases on our renovated units, we ask what the impact of these variables will be on our returns.

For example, let's say the goal is to hit a 1.75 multiple: if you invest $10 million, then your goal is $17.5 million on the principal, or equity capital, you invested. Suppose the deal seems good, it's a great location, and the area is developing but not very fast. We run the numbers in our underwriting model and see what the deal will look like in seven to ten years. If the underwriting model shows that after seven years the deal is a 1.75 multiple, then we know we will still have the desired return after seven years even if the deal doesn't yield the projected return on shorter-term holds.

One way to handle downsides is to have a backup plan that transforms the downside into something with upside. Stress testing a model enables you to develop backup plans that have a good chance of succeeding. We stress test for increases in interest rates, tax increases, decreases in rent, lower occupancy rates—all our key performance indicators. We stress test the underwriting model's metrics aggressively against the worst-case scenario.

Suppose you got a floating-rate loan, even though the forecast, which is based on what is happening in the market, says interest rates will go up by half a point the next year. We stress test our underwriting model by making the increase 1 percent instead of the forecast half a point. With this assumption in the underwriting model, we know that the deal still makes sense if interest rates rise by half a point or more, up to 1 percent.

How do we take property taxes into account? Texas is a nondisclosure state, meaning you don't have to disclose the purchase price of a property, so a county's valuation of the property will likely be different from the amount you acquired the property for. At the time of purchase, we wouldn't know the exact amount of property taxes for the coming year. This is especially so when ownership of the property changes because it triggers a property tax reassessment. The chances of property taxes going up is high. To account for this unknown, we underwrite the deal as if real estate taxes have gone up to 80 to 100 percent of our purchase price depending on which county the property is in. Even though there is a low chance that there will be a large tax increase, we want to have that cushion.

We also stress test a rent increase assumption in the underwriting model. Let's say our plan is to increase rent by $100 after we do an upgrade. Instead, our underwriting model assumes a rent increase of

$75. Then we know that if we can't raise rents by $100, the deal will still work. We also evaluate what will happen to the bottom line if the occupancy is not as high as we projected.

Another way to deal with a present downside or one that crops up after you've closed a deal is to be flexible. When you are flexible with a deal's timing and other variables, you can overcome the possibilities.

Using Flexibility to Overcome Downsides

You might think that the easiest way to create flexibility in real estate is through adjusting the timing of a deal. Are property prices low right now? Hold on to the property and sell later. Are interest rates rising? Wait for them to fall. Do property prices seem to be peaking? Sell sooner rather than wait. There's flexibility when we sell, and there's flexibility with how long we hold on to a property. However, there are other ways to generate flexibility.

RECAPITALIZING A DEAL

Recapitalizing a deal is a way to generate flexibility. With most of the Fannie Mae and Freddie Mac fixed- or floating-rate loans, you have an option to refinance and obtain a supplemental loan after a year of holding the property, provided your property has increased in value. For example, let's say we bought a property for $10 million with a $6.5 million loan and $3.5 million of equity capital. We also invested $2 million on improvements, which the bank was willing to finance at the same 65/35 percentage split ($1.3 million loan and $700,000 in equity). This puts the total capitalization at a $7.8 million loan ($6.5 million from the purchase price + $1.3 million from improvements) and $4.2 million in equity ($3.5 million from the purchase price + $700,000 from improvements). A year from now, the property value is higher, say $14 million, so you can obtain a supplemental loan up to 70 (or 75) percent of the new value, which is $9.8 million. Now you could pull out $2 million, and your equity investment would become only $2.2 million compared to the original $4.2 million. This new financial position comes with an increase in monthly loan payments, which are based on current interest rates on the additional $2 million borrowed.

Why would we recapitalize? There are two reasons: it boosts returns and reduces risk. Let's say we're expecting a 20 percent IRR on a property, and it's not working as well as we had planned in the underwriting model. Suppose we bought the property for $10 million, invested $2 million on improvements, and the value has gone up. Now we can go back to the lender and ask for a supplemental loan of $2 million to recapitalize. By taking on additional debt, we can send money back to the investors earlier than planned and increase the project's IRR because IRRs are time driven (see earlier discussion). After recapitalization, your investment in the property is lower because you get some of your equity back. We are invested in the deal at a lower basis, but our return profile in the long run is the same or has even gone up. The result is that we make sure our principal is not at risk or, at least, our returns are higher on the money we invested.

Taking on additional debt through recapitalization and using the funds to reduce the amount of equity in a project serves to reduce the amount of risk a project has. In this example, the equity balance decreases by almost 50 percent, from about $4.2 million to $2.2 million (these are simplified numbers). As we explained earlier, these are nonrecourse loans, so if the project fails, your risk is limited to losing your equity. Thus recapitalization in this example reduces your risk by close to 50 percent.

You can always get a supplemental loan on Fannie Mae and Freddie Mac loans, but getting the loan depends on having more revenue coming in from the property. The NOI always determines the value of the property.

The benefit of a refinance cash-out is that you get back some of the principal you put into the deal. Now you have those funds to use in another deal or for anything else in your life. This gives you great flexibility when a deal is good or when you're faced with a downside.

CHANGING THE COURSE OF A REHABILITATION PROJECT

Another way to turn around a downside is by changing the course of a rehabilitation project. We set up a deal with the goal of putting, say, $2 million into renovations—$1 million on the exterior and $1 million on the interior. Suppose the cost to renovate each unit was $5,000 to $6,000, but we did not get the kind of rent increase that we expected. Instead of renovating all the units, we decided to shift some of the money into a renovation that would have more impact. On this property, each unit had a small yard but was without a fence. So we used the interior renovation money to put a fence around the yards, a good option for pet owners. Now each apartment had a private yard, which enabled us to capture the higher rent. Plus, we could charge a $100 fee for having a pet.

Once you implement a business plan and learn it is not generating the revenue that you expected, you need to be flexible about your next steps. In this case, before implementing the process, we felt a certain outcome would happen. Halfway through the process, we realized the money was not being used in a worthwhile way. At that point, you need to change course and do something else that will generate more revenue.

Another lesson is that you need to evaluate your plan against reality. Reality may not be what you thought it would be. If you're flexible, you can capitalize on that. You don't just do something and move on without evaluating.

COURSE CORRECTING WHEN THINGS GO WRONG

When things go wrong, you are no longer in the territory of a downside. Something fundamental and unforeseen can happen. Now you're already in a deal, and it's not turning out the way your underwriting model suggested it would.

For example, one of our deals in Dallas, a 254-unit complex, was not generating the kind of revenue we expected. In addition, when the contractors were doing the exterior renovation work, they discovered issues with the foundation. There was a crack, and water was seeping in. You can't rent units with water damage, and you need to prevent further damage. During our due diligence process, the inspection reports did not catch the problem. Whether you caught it or not before buying it, once you own it, you must fix it; if you don't, you will have bigger issues in the future. So instead of renovating 50 percent of the units as planned, we renovated only 40 percent. We shifted funds to repair the foundation of the building.

This was a learning experience. At the time we bought this property, our standard practice was to visit 33 percent of the units and then extrapolate. Most of the time, you rely on your own teams; they may be good, but they may not be experts like civil engineers are. Now we hire an expert company that visits all the buildings and all the units. Had we hired that company in the past, we would have caught the foundation problems that a property inspector missed.

Today, we have checks and balances in place to avoid similar mistakes. We cross-check the experts' work with our independent contractors' rehab scope of work. We also read all the reports under a microscope. And we make sure the acquisitions team interacts with the asset management team to coordinate all these efforts so that nobody misses anything.

EXPERIENCE WITH DOWNSIDES BUILDS EXPERTISE

This case in which we missed problems with the foundation illustrates a critically important point. Downsides that you must resolve through a course correction are opportunities to learn. If you just view the downside as a mistake and move on, you miss out on the value of the experience. To turn failures or downsides into something positive, you must pause and reflect, critically analyze your failures, apply what you learn, and build expertise. By analyzing what led us to miss the damaged foundation, we built expertise. As a result, we instituted a different process for evaluating properties.

> TO TURN FAILURES OR DOWNSIDES INTO SOMETHING POSITIVE, YOU MUST PAUSE AND REFLECT, CRITICALLY ANALYZE YOUR FAILURES, APPLY WHAT YOU LEARN, AND BUILD EXPERTISE.

In addition to events that are external to your firm's core business processes, downsides and failures can occur inside your organization. These can have effects far beyond their immediate impact. Overlooking the composition of your team is a downside that has this broader effect.

The corollary of achieving more with teamwork (see chapter 3) is that one weak team member can wreak havoc. Weak team members can often be the result of a leader's not wanting to pay high salaries for experience. When the fear that a high salary will add overhead outweighs the risk of hiring inexperienced people, you set yourself up for teams that can't deliver high-quality results.

We run a lean team. The more experience we have on board, the higher the chance we will make the best deals. But our leadership team is human. Just like most people, we want to avoid risk. So, until we learned to do better, we avoided risking high overhead and hired people with less experience. We learned the hard way that you must set compensation high to get the best talent.

When you hire inexperienced people, they often end up learning in the field. Unless they come in at a junior level or as an intern, people on staff should know how to perform in their roles. In commercial real estate, it is important to hire people with the exact experience you need.

In the cases that follow, the inexperienced employees are intelligent and hard workers; their inexperience in commercial real estate implies nothing about their work ethic or talent. When we hired individuals with experience in a different industry and new to the commercial real estate industry, their lack of direct experience created a vacuum; eventually, someone else had to perform their roles. The extra work creates a burden on experienced team members, which produces resentment. Three cases illustrate the potential problems and a counterexample.

One employee's experience was managing loans for lenders, not managing properties. Although lenders have loans on properties, they visit a property only infrequently; their concern is consistently receiving the loan payment, not how well the property performs. Because of his former experience, this employee did not visit properties often enough, performance decreased, and the properties no longer produced the NOI we projected in the underwriting model. By the time we learned of the problem, occupancy fell from 90 to 70 percent. We spent a year course correcting this downside. Luckily, our effort to mitigate the fault paid off; we are selling the property when the market is still good.

In another case, we hired the relative of a team member. Initially, an experienced team member had to teach the new employee basics as well as advanced critical procedures. The learning curve can be steep. Once the inexperienced employee learned his roles, his performance improved. However, the training took a toll on the experienced team member, and the result caused irreparable damage.

A third case serves as a counterexample. We have also hired extremely talented people with tremendous experience in acquisitions. Because one of these experienced people had acquired properties in commercial real estate many times, he ran the entire acquisition process of buying a big portfolio. His performance yielded returns beyond our strict underwriting criteria. Because one individual ran that deal, we were able to focus on making other profitable deals.

We used a thorough vetting process to hire this team member after screening many résumés and interviewing a few competitive candidates. We did not apply this vetting process when we hired a business partner's family member or an employee without the needed experience. When you hire for experience and compensate adequately, everyone wins.

The contrast in experiences built our hiring expertise. Now we know that we should fear and avoid hiring inexperienced people and embrace the benefits of rewarding expertise with higher salaries.

HIRING THE RIGHT PEOPLE IS COMPARABLE TO EXECUTING THE RIGHT DEAL.

Whether your organization is a small team, like ours, or a large multidivision corporation, whom you hire can have downsides that are best to avoid, rather than correct after the fact.

The guidance that buying right is important but execution is everything led me to create a very effective asset management team for American Ventures. Hiring the right people is comparable to executing the right deal.

Learning from Outliers

Many of the downside cases I have reviewed to this point are outliers—extremely rare positive or negative events. Most cases of downsides are outliers. We rarely find that properties have cracks in the foundation after we buy them. We rarely hire the wrong person for the job. Being at the right place at the right time to buy land near the Formula 1 racetrack in Austin was a rare experience. We rarely misidentify the path of gentrification. We look at these rare cases to learn. It is easier to learn from mistakes than from successes, where the lessons are subtler.

We usually invest in areas we are very familiar with. During our initial growth, our focus has been mostly the major primary and secondary markets of Austin, Dallas, Houston, and San Antonio, Texas, and some nearby locations. We know this area best—the different neighborhoods, the submarkets, the expected paths of gentrification, what industries are moving into the area, and so on. However, when we heard about a low-price deal in the Tulsa, Oklahoma, market, we decided that at such a low price, we really could not go wrong.

The market fundamentals were good, but we had no physical experience in the area. In earlier chapters, I made the point about how important it is to have boots on the ground and acquire properties that our team can visit regularly. But in this case, all the indicators said the multifamily market was increasing in Tulsa. We followed what I call a macrostrategy; the macroeconomic indicators in the Tulsa area—for example, low unemployment rate, increasing employment, lower consumer price index than in the overall United States, and so on—were good. But we should have looked closer at the submarket; the economic indicators in our submarket were not as good as in the general Tulsa area.

We did a lot of research on Tulsa and found the city was putting money into the area. We spoke to the city manager, who gave decent information on the area and the city's plans. We thought the city's investment was a positive. But we did not know that historically the city left these three blocks out of its development plans. Even though we delivered a good housing product, people didn't want to live in these three blocks and would not pay higher rent. You can't change the demographic profile of a neighborhood. In commercial real estate, your job is not to engage in urban planning and change neighborhoods.

This was an outlier because we ignored our own advice and did not stick to the basics. If you want to invest in a property, you must look at it and its surrounding environment. It's important to avoid being too aggressive on rent growths in areas that are historically left behind. When your plans depend on city funding to improve pockets of a town, expect that process to take longer than what city officials project. Most importantly, invest in properties that your asset management team can visit frequently. This is true even for a property with a low price in a market that you want to break into.

Outlier investments can occur in markets that have high growth. Austin is one of the fastest-growing cities in the United States; however, it is notorious for taking twelve to eighteen months to grant site plans and building permits. We were confident that we had a property in a great location, very close to downtown, and that we could reduce that time from eighteen months to nine months. Other professionals advised that we shouldn't count on getting permits in nine months. Our plan for the property was to transform it into a thirty-unit luxury condominium building, and our colleagues said we might not be able to get approval for it at all. But we thought that with an exceptional location already zoned for housing development, we could have a fast-track permitting process. We were overconfident because we did not know the level of bureaucratic red tape in the city. I learned that anything requiring a majority vote from a planning commission is controversial.

The land itself had some troubling issues, including a floodplain and drainage easement. One-third of the land couldn't be developed at all. However, an expert development team with professionals who are specialists in urban core development sites can build amazing structures even on sites with floodplain issues. A development team includes civil engineers, architects, and mechanical, electrical, and plumbing engineers.

The three controversies in this area were primarily between the needs of future residents and the extended neighborhood. The first neighborhood controversy revolved around the zoning for high-density housing. The development was desirable for future residents because it would provide luxury housing near downtown where people worked. Any residential unit in a downtown or central business district is expensive to rent. We planned our site to be a great deal: only one mile from the city center—a two-minute drive to downtown—with rents almost half as expensive as comparable downtown areas. But the extended neighborhood did not want high-density buildings in their area.

A second issue was affordability. In the normal course of business, financial considerations mean that you can't provide more than 10 percent affordable units without grants. If you develop a high-density structure—for example, a thirty-unit condominium building on a half-acre site zoned for a five-story building—the city requires that 10 percent of the units be affordable; no affordability requirement applies to lower-density structures—say, a nineteen-unit, three-story condominium building. Our underwriting model could accommodate 10 percent, but the extended neighborhood wanted 40 percent. They claimed to have struck a deal with the previous developer for 40 percent affordable units, which was never recorded. In our feasibility study, we found no records of 40 percent affordability agreements. If we found such an agreement, the site would not have been viable. City staff confirmed that we needed only 10 percent affordable units in a five-story, thirty-unit building.

The third issue was providing a convenient path for public access to nearby transportation. Owners of nearby single-family homes did not want a public access walkway so close to their property lines or in front of their driveways.

Our development plans addressed all three issues. Nevertheless, the extended neighborhood raised concerns.

The land zoned for development included a park of historic significance, confirmed by an expert, where African Americans held an annual Juneteenth celebration in honor of the Emancipation Proclamation. The city tried to buy the property, which changed hands many times during the twentieth century, to preserve its historical value but did not have the funds. The cause of freedom is very dear to me, and I am a big fan of enhancing neighborhood values and honoring historic significance. Therefore, our development plans included using our own funds to build a public park with a memorial plaque, whether we built a nineteen-unit building or a thirty-unit building. People would be able to hang out in this park without disturbing the building's residents.

We could build a nineteen-unit building with no affordable housing requirement or a thirty-unit high-density building with 10 percent affordable units. But the extended neighborhood insisted on 40 percent.

We had our architects plan for public access in a way that would protect current residents' privacy. It required people to walk an extra block, but we thought the trade-off was to residents' and the neighborhood's benefit. Again, the extended neighborhood disagreed with the plan.

It seemed to us that the neighborhood organization's goal was to prevent the development from happening. However, they could not do so because of the city's zoning.

Our plan came to the planning commission several times throughout this process. They required that we resolve the issues with the neighborhood before they would vote. When the plans finally came to a vote, we lost six to five; some of our allies were not present at the meeting when the vote was taken. In the end, prospective residents, the extended neighborhood, and my firm all lost. Instead of constructing a thirty-unit, five-story building, we now have shovel-ready land with an approved site plan and building permits for a nineteen-unit, three-story building.

I expected this development to be straightforward, but it was not. I didn't foresee how politics would affect the complexity. For our company, it was a negative outlier. The lesson seems obvious: it is not effective to spend eighteen months or more trying to develop a small building.

Although you can use time and financial adjustments to turn many downsides into profitable upsides, the only value you gain from some negative outliers is knowledge and experience. Armed with this knowledge and experience and with expert team members, American Ventures is well positioned to overcome any challenges when we meet them again.

EXECUTIVE SUMMARY

- Understand the distinction between downsides—issues that can be spotted in advance and addressed with a course correction—and threats—issues you cannot identify in advance.

- Analyze the risks inherent in being the first to upgrade a property in a distressed area or path of gentrification.

- Always stress test underwriting models rigorously and especially for variations in timing.

- Use stress testing to devise backup plans to course correct for downsides.

- Use flexible timing, recapitalization, and changes to rehabilitation plans to address downsides as they occur.

- When threats occur, use them to learn how to adjust your standard practices to avoid future threats.

- Be aware that downsides and threats can exist within your organization and team as well as in external assets.

- Employ a strict vetting process and pay at or above industry standards when making new hires to avoid the costly mistakes of inexperienced team members.

- Identify situations that are likely outliers, and take a cautious approach to engaging with them. Deals with political qualities are frequently outliers and might require more resources than is worthwhile.

CHAPTER 6

ASK REALLY GOOD QUESTIONS AND DELEGATE TO EXPERTS

The Importance of Curiosity

W hen I worked as a pharmaceutical scientist and first had money to invest, I wondered what the best investment was. I saw people around me investing in real estate, asked my friends some questions about what they were doing, and then just leapt into my first deal. I had some success, but I was doing the same thing as a lot of other people. So I wondered what I could do differently to distinguish myself from the others. I innovated and had some success. But then I wondered how I could achieve more.

You might see the pattern here: curiosity and leaping in feetfirst. Curiosity and boldness are helpful in entrepreneurship, but they will take you only so far.

When I wanted to become a good public speaker, rather than having someone coach me, I took a lot of speaking engagements. Speaking engagements are a great way to get exposure and move an entrepreneurial venture forward. However, I realized that I was doing what I had always done: learning by doing, one of the fundamentals of entrepreneurial success. I also thought about what happens when you do the same thing: you get the same results. My curiosity led me to wonder what would happen if I tried a different approach.

Soon, I realized that a better approach would balance learning by doing with having a coach. The research on this topic shows that directed practice with a coach will get you to an expert level faster than practice without a coach.[10] After working with a coach, which is essentially what TED fellowships do for people, when I present at speaking engagements, I hope to have a greater measure of confidence and success.

My speaking topic, of course, is multifamily and commercial real estate. I talk most often about an entrepreneurial approach to real estate investment, and I always tell people to stick to the basics. One of the genuinely useful basics is to be curious. If you are curious about the fundamentals, like a scientist, you will develop many ideas naturally. Learning from the fundamentals and from experts gives you a boost and traction in whatever you do because you don't have to reinvent the wheel. Knowing the fundamentals of your field—whatever that

---

10   Daniel Goleman, *Focus: The Hidden Driver of Excellence* (New York: Harper, 2013); Anders Ericsson, "Episode 147: Anders Ericsson—What Malcolm Gladwell Got Wrong About the 10,000 Hour Rule," in *The Learning Leaders*, hosted by Ryan Hawk, episode 147, podcast, MP3 audio, 49:06, August 3, 2016, https://learning-leader.com/episode-147-anders-ericsson/.

field is—enables you to work and ask questions at a higher level than you would otherwise be able to do.

Accelerated Intelligence

Curiosity will take you far, sometimes into territory you might not otherwise explore. But there are learning techniques that can boost what you gain from curiosity. One set of techniques is called accelerated intelligence, and it can also increase your capacity to ask good questions. Elon Musk uses accelerated intelligence techniques. Charlie Munger, who is Warren Buffett's business partner, does it. Ray Dalio does it.

Michael Simmons, the guru of accelerated intelligence, explains how these cutting-edge entrepreneurs use a handful of techniques to learn across industries, learn fast, and apply what they learn. It seems extraordinary, but anyone can do it.

First, you need to practice what Simmons calls the five-hour rule: spend a minimum of five hours a week learning. Second, spend your study time learning different fields, and study each enough that you can understand the basic principles. Elon Musk says that learning the fundamentals of a field is more important than learning all the details. Simmons recommends building mental models of the fundamental principles. Third, compare and contrast the basic principles (or your mental models of them) to identify similarities across the fields. To develop innovations and breakthrough ideas, apply what you learn to your field.[11]

---

11 Michael Simmons, "How Elon Musk Learns Faster and Better than Everyone Else," *Accelerated Intelligence*, December 8, 2018, https://medium.com/accelerated-intelligence/learn-like-elon-musk-fe8f8da6137c.

Michael Simmons, "5-Hour Rule: If You're Not Spending 5 Hours Per Week

If you think you don't have time to practice the five-hour rule, consider that professionals in many fields—doctors, nurses, management analysts, lawyers, pharmacists, secondary school teachers, and others—must take a certain number of continuing education hours each year to maintain their professional standing.

Elon Musk is a great example of what you can accomplish if you devote yourself to accelerated intelligence. His successful companies—many of them have broken new ground—span the financial industry, transportation, artificial intelligence, and space travel.

Some people call learning across different fields intellectual cross-pollination. The key is to focus on identifying the basics and observing the similarities and differences. Applying what you learn from multiple fields will lead you to ask good questions in your field.

Qualities Entrepreneurs Have in Common: Grit and Flexibility

Many people assume that entrepreneurs are extroverts or like to take risks. I have a spirit of adventure, and people might think that is also a quality of entrepreneurs. But I have interacted with many people, and entrepreneurs have as many different characteristics as you can think of. There is not one specific way to be an entrepreneur. Some are adventurous like me, and some are not. Some are extroverts, some are introverts, and some are a little of both.

Nevertheless, entrepreneurs have many qualities in common. One is curiosity. Another is grit. A third is flexibility. When I observe what entrepreneurs do, the qualities that help them most are grit

Learning, You're Being Irresponsible," *Accelerated Intelligence*, October 12, 2017, https://medium.com/accelerated-intelligence/the-5-hour-rule-if-youre-not-spending-5-hours-per-week-learning-you-re-being-irresponsible-791c3f18f5e6.

and flexibility.

Curiosity, flexibility, and grit work together to keep a person moving forward toward his or her goals. It seems to be a self-driving cycle. Curiosity will draw you toward something. When challenges occur—and they always do—grit kicks in and keeps you engaged and moving forward. As circumstances change—and they always do—flexibility enables you to reevaluate and pivot as necessary. If there is an obstacle that you cannot remove, flexibility and grit will enable you to move around it. And curiosity helps you discover how to move around obstacles.

CURIOUSITY LEADS TO DISCOVERY AND DRAWS YOU IN

GRIT KICKS IN WHEN CHALLENGES COME UP

FLEXIBILITY ENABLES YOU TO REEVALUATE AND PIVOT

FLEXIBILITY AND GRIT ENABLE YOU TO MOVE AROUND OBSTACLES

Enabling Objectives and Key Results to Propel Your Curiosity and Action

Curiosity is about learning, and the more you learn the more curious you become. Buying a property, discovering it had buildings with cracks in the foundation, and having to shift plans and renovation funds made what looked like a simple deal into a more complex situation. (See chapter 5 for the whole story.) When we evaluated what went wrong on that deal, the biggest lesson was that walking through 33 percent of the units and extrapolating isn't enough. The lesson taught us that we needed to learn about the entire property.

There is a downside to curiosity: it can lead you to focus on too much learning. And if you spend too much time on learning, analysis paralysis may set in. When that happens, you may not spend enough time on doing or ever get around to doing. The antidote to getting stuck in the learning cycle is to always keep the end in mind. When you focus on your goal, you can balance curiosity and learning with doing.

Objectives and key results (OKRs)—John Doerr describes this technique in *Measure What Matters*, and I discuss its application to American Ventures in chapters 7 and 8—can play a significant role in staying focused rather than allowing curiosity to distract you.[12] When I don't see a key result, I know that I'm deviating, maybe overdoing, analysis because I'm not in the range of my target. The best way to state an objective or goal is in a way that you can measure. For example, my current goal might be to acquire many deals. Many is a generic goal; you can't measure it, so

THE BEST WAY TO STATE AN OBJECTIVE OR GOAL IS IN A WAY THAT YOU CAN MEASURE.

---

12 John Doerr, *Measure What Matters: How Google, Bono, and the Gates Foundation Rock the World with OKRs.* (New York: Portfolio/Penguin, 2018).

you can't know when you are near your target. A better goal is to acquire 3,000 units in the next six months; now you have a measurable goal. If you're deviating from the key number of 3,000 units, then you're wandering around. Maybe you are curious about too many potential deals. The time frame is equally important. If six months have gone by and it is taking closer to nine months to acquire 3,000 units, then I am also not sticking to the target. Maybe I am spending too much time learning about and analyzing too many deals in the pipeline.

To reach your goals, you need to be disciplined about following your plans and disciplined about evaluating whether you're on track. Because commercial real estate moves very fast, I evaluate every day as well as take action toward my goals; that's my style. But I am aware that evaluating every day might be too much. You can't get to the result if you're evaluating but not doing. A more measured approach is to evaluate how you're tracking toward goals every quarter or every two quarters.

It is critical to bring everyone who is part of your team into the evaluation loop. Team members should have individual goals that derive from your goals. In addition, your goals and team members' goals should be public. This gives everyone a common platform. When everyone freely shares their goals, it develops a sense of accountability while reinforcing discipline. With a common platform and public goals, everyone from the top of the organization to the bottom is in the limelight with measured goals.

One question for the CEO or lead partner in a firm to consider is what to be disciplined about. I think discipline for the CEO or partner is best applied to achieving key results. Being disciplined about day-to-day activities is useful only when the activity feeds into achieving key results. For example, emails can be a distraction unless you identify and only look at those that are critical and important to the deal you are working on. Technology, like customer relationship management software, can help leverage your focus, even in commercial real estate.

Commercial real estate deals require a lot of relationship building with investors as well as touring properties. In addition, when you are trying to scale your business, it is important to spend time among people who can teach you. This means being out of the office half of the time and being flexible to take advantage of opportunities that provide access to the top people in your field.

But being in the office only half the time has a downside. If the head of an organization is not around, maybe the team is not as focused. Counterbalancing the idea that the leader ensures focus is the idea that things should happen no matter where the leader is. I set expectations with my team that help them work independently. Because my team knows working independently is an expectation, they engage in the activities that produce key results.

This ties back to hiring for experience and expertise. When you hire experts, it becomes easy to delegate to them. When you can delegate critical tasks and be confident team members will produce high-quality results, it frees your time to explore future ventures. When you leave completely capable people to do their work independently, they work to their strengths, which enables you to work to your strengths.

It is not so much that you cultivate curiosity as that you create the right circumstances for curiosity to flourish. Those circumstances include taking a thoughtful approach to what you do, evaluating continually to keep yourself on track, delegating critical tasks to highly competent team members and trusting them to do a good job, and working to your strengths so that you can devote time to future ventures.

How to Convert a Fear into a Strength

Part of working to your strengths involves turning your attention inward and evaluating what works for you. Although you can take tests that provide information about strengths, a more organic approach works as well, perhaps better. You will become conscious of your strengths if you spend some time thoughtfully evaluating what you are doing to reach your goals in life.

YOU WILL BECOME CONSCIOUS OF YOUR STRENGTHS IF YOU SPEND SOME TIME THOUGHTFULLY EVALUATING WHAT YOU ARE DOING TO REACH YOUR GOALS IN LIFE.

Consider that Bill Gates learns well from reading; he says he reads about fifty books a year and enjoys learning that way. His learning technique makes me think that I should read more books. Not reading has some significant costs. For one thing, it is challenging to practice the five-hour rule of accelerated intelligence without reading. I could overcome weak reading by listening to audiobooks. However, I know I learn best from talking with people. My strength lies in spending time with an author, asking thoughtful questions, and listening to the answers.

The essence of mitigating weak reading by discussing books with their authors is developing an ally relationship.

When I meet with an author, I might ask him or her to give me the nuts and bolts of their thoughts. If I have a specific question, I ask it; sometimes I have been fortunate to spend a day with an author on just that one specific question. Asking questions lets authors know you recognize the value of their ideas. When you seek out the author to learn from them personally, it inspires them to give thoughtful and considered answers; most authors are generous with their basic ideas. If I can't meet the author, I read a summary of the book that focuses on its premise. Either way, I get the information I need. But talking with the experts makes learning fun for me and helps me build connections and alliances.

In fact, it is possible to mitigate the costs of any weakness by working with allies whose strengths complement your weaknesses.

EXECUTIVE SUMMARY

- Let curiosity guide you to explore possibilities outside your routine way of thinking. Ask questions that begin with "I wonder what would happen if … " and "I wonder how … "

- Use accelerated intelligence techniques to come up with innovative approaches.

- Spend at least five hours a week learning something new.

- Develop and practice grit and flexibility.

- Keep your goal in mind in order to avoid getting caught in a learning cycle or overanalysis.

- Commit to being disciplined in working toward your goals and evaluating your progress.

- Use objectives and key results to make sure your objectives are well articulated, your tactics are spelled out, and your actions are time bound.

- Use frequent reflection to evaluate what you are doing to reach your goals in life and understand how to use your strengths to mitigate your weaknesses.

CHAPTER 7

NETWORKING AND GIVING BACK: CREATING A CENTER OF INFLUENCE

When I grew up in India, my father often told me to always make good use of my time. So when I found myself with time on my hands in the evenings after work, I tried different ways to generate other income. My time in network marketing taught me the power of leverage. I thought about following my interests in business and the pharmaceutical industry and starting a pharmaceutical company, but I could not do that from home in my spare time in a world of Pfizers and Mercks. Beyond that, none of these ideas appealed to me until I started investing in real estate. Making real estate deals was fun, and I found a way to help people while I made a little money. In the back of my mind, also because of my father's example, was the question:

What am I doing with my life?

When I partnered with an expert on zero-down real estate investing in single-family homes, I learned more from this experience than how to invest in real estate effectively and scale what I was doing. First, I learned that if you seek out someone to learn from, you can find that person; researching what you need makes a difference. Second, I learned that your reputation matters. These are three essential factors in networking: build a reputation for serious and good work, seek out expertise that can support your ventures, and deliver on your end of the bargain.

Whom You Hang Out with Influences How Your Life Goes

One consistent lesson my experiences taught me is that being diligent and systematic about what you do leads to success most of the time. In science, you get the clearest results from diligent research and systematic experimentation. In commercial real estate, you make the best deals from diligent research and a systematic underwriting process. It is the same in life. A diligent and systematic approach to what you do yields results.

Consider your inner circle, the people you spend the most time hanging out with. There were years in which I didn't associate much with folks who were more successful than me. My circle was a group of individuals who had great educations, earned $100,000 to $500,000 a year, led a decent life, but didn't think about accomplishing more. There was no vision to achieve wealth—which is an engine for doing good in the world—and pass it on to future generations. I was complacent, not goal driven, and at a plateau in my life. At times, I was the smartest in the group, which did not help me push myself forward. But the lack of focus on wealth jolted me out of complacency. It was the opposite of what I observed while growing up.

LET YOUR VALUES GUIDE YOUR NETWORKING

Those years of complacency taught me the truth of what my father always said:

- Never settle for less in life.

- Fight all the odds to achieve what you want.

- Achieve tremendously in life, not just financially.

- Educate underprivileged kids.

- Have quality and good taste in anything you do.

- Make good use of your time.

By focusing on wealth, I can put all my father's guidance into action. His guidance is a refined approach that fosters staying grounded, taking care of family, and supporting the community.

One way to make sure you live your values and use your time well is to belong to a circle of like-minded people. Like others, my first attempt was to build this circle around my career. Initially, I joined an organization focused on entrepreneurship; it consisted of entrepreneurs who are founders of companies meeting a certain revenue threshold. I learned a lot, was motivated to seek success, and benefited from the power of associating with entrepreneurs who excelled. Although it immediately relieved my sense of complacency, I was not confident and happy in that organization. Something was missing.

The essence of the values my father passed on is to excel in personal, professional, and philanthropic endeavors. These are the three pillars of life, and they are like concentric circles, moving further away from yourself at the center. To date, my objectives have been to achieve scale in the professional circle, which has led to entrepreneurial success. But I want to focus on more than professional success. Having an inner circle—a close network—that focuses on personal and philanthropic objectives, as well as career, helps manifest these values in life. To move beyond professional success, I knew I needed to create or find that like-minded network. I want to associate myself with people who are authorities in their professional fields and are authoritative in their personal and philanthropic endeavors.

Creating a network is often misconstrued as being solely focused on career and being transactional. Before you ask someone for what you need—an introduction, recommendation, or job—you must give them something they value. But if you maintain relationships at a transactional level, the trust that enables you to be vulnerable is unlikely to emerge. Without vulnerability, you are unlikely to develop deep connections with others.[13] And without those deep connections,

WITHOUT VULNERABILITY, YOU ARE UNLIKELY TO DEVELOP DEEP CONNECTIONS WITH OTHERS.

you are unlikely to create the network of friends and trusted confidants—in twenty-first century words, your tribe—that is crucial to accomplishing amazing things in your personal and professional endeavors.

Recognizing that I needed to be equally concerned with developing the personal and philanthropic circles in addition to career led me to an investment club called The Investment Group for Enhanced Results in the 21st Century (TIGER 21). I was thinking about the big questions—what am I doing with my life and how do I want to live

---

13   Brené Brown, *Daring Greatly: How the Courage to Be Vulnerable Transforms the Way We Live, Love, Parent, and Lead* (New York: Avery, 2012).

my life?—and the organization's goals are increasing wealth, working toward self-actualization, and giving back to the community through philanthropy—my three pillars of life.

A benefit of TIGER 21 is that it pushes me to accomplish more. For example, I believe I am less knowledgeable and successful than others in my chapter and think I have much more to do. There is no room for complacency here. Spending time with people who are more successful than me motivates me and helps me create a vision to achieve more. In anything, whether it's financial or personal success, people who are doing better than you will bring you along with them.

To become a member of TIGER 21, you need to meet a net worth threshold. The other members of this organization are successful. They are entrepreneurs who have made their businesses happen; they are not in the process of trying to make them happen. That they have successfully created entrepreneurial businesses is extremely important for me because I want to surround myself with people who have made it. Every member is aiming for the next level. If you think in terms of Maslow's hierarchy, members are working toward self-actualization. It is inspiring to be in a room where everyone is on the path to self-actualization.

But, after all, we are all human beings, and we have the same issues. In a way, members of this group have passed through the training process. Consequently, no one is trying to sell anything. Everyone is sharing their ideas and principles. You literally have the board of directors for your life. We meet once a month, and a chapter chair facilitates the meetings. There are several chapters across the US, Canada, UK, and, more recently, Hong Kong. Thus it gives us exposure to national and international members bound by common principles. Although throughout the year each member presents and defends their investment portfolio within their chapter during what's called Portfolio Defense, personal growth and philanthropy are at the forefront. In many respects, we've taken care of Maslow's basics for ourselves and our families.

There are not many organizations for entrepreneurs, and most of them are deal-centric and focused on business creation and growth. In contrast, TIGER 21 focuses on wealth creation across generations. The organization encourages you to think about the future of your family, your community, and the broader global community around you. The focus on wealth generation and philanthropy gives a tremendous return on investment. It forces you to set midrange—one to two years—and long-range—four to five years or beyond—goals. That goal setting and advance thinking is priceless.

THE BENEFITS OF FINDING YOUR TRIBE

Making your key results public and communicating with the people in your network about your objectives helps you benefit from a trusted inner circle. Once you go public with your goals, it is harder to let them languish.

John Doerr's description of the objectives and key results (OKRs) system that propelled Intel (where the system was developed by Andy Grove), Google, an array of tech start-ups, the Bill & Melinda Gates Foundation, and Bono's DATA (Debt, AIDS, Trade, Africa) organization and One Campaign is inspiring. The idea is simple: state "tangible, objective, and unambiguous" goals whose achievement is easy to identify; and state key results that "express measurable milestones which, if achieved, will advance objectives in a useful manner … "[14] and that "describe outcomes … that include evidence of completion." OKRs give an organization or individual focus, commitment to

---

14   John Doerr, *Measure What Matters: How Google, Bono, and the Gates Foundation Rock the World with OKRs.* (New York: Portfolio/Penguin, 2018), 256–257.

priorities, alignment with goals, the connection that enables teamwork, and a way to track progress and hold yourself and others accountable. All these capabilities are equally important to success.

What appealed to me most were the OKR qualities that lead to transparency and accountability. They support my idea that going public with your goals has many benefits. For example, a few years ago, I told my inner circle when my company hit the milestone of owning one thousand multifamily units. I also told them my goal was to get to four to seven thousand units. Fast-forward three years, and I reached my goal of owning four thousand units in the multifamily space. If I wasn't surrounded with people who were able to hear what I said without jealousy or competitiveness, and if I wasn't able to hold myself accountable, achieving that milestone would have been more difficult.

My next goal is to find a long-term mentor, an individual who is both a successful game changer in the real estate industry and accomplished in personal and philanthropic endeavors. I hope to create a win-win opportunity with this individual and reach his or her level of accomplishment in the next five or ten years. For many years, I have been working on my own without advice or feedback on how to reach my next objective. To acquire the kind of forthright feedback and thoughtful advice that will help me create the circumstances to get to the next milestone, I need to put myself in the right place at the right time to connect with an ally who complements my strengths. To make this connection, I will reach out to my network and let people know that I'm looking for a mentor. I'm sure my network will lead me to two or three people who can give me good advice, and then I'll work more closely with one of them.

Finding the right mentor is one way I measure how well I am reaching my objectives. Mentors invest their time, knowledge, and reputation in you. So when you reach out to find a mentor, you need to have the credibility that you will be a good investment, a good mentee. In addition to working through my network, I'll develop an idea of what I'm looking for, evaluate whether a prospective mentor has it, and evaluate whether I am eligible to be a good mentee for him or her. Likewise, a mentor will be evaluating whether I'm worth the investment—whether I have a reputation as someone who can deliver results and reflect positively on him or her. My reputation and credibility are only two things I bring to a mentoring relationship. I believe that, like any deal, a mentoring relationship must be a win for both parties.

The idea that whom you hang out with influences how your life goes is a story about how success breeds success. One facet of all success stories is that success requires that you be thoughtful, diligent, and systematic. That is as true about choosing your inner circle as it is about the rest of your business efforts. If you want to be successful, you must decide that you are going to be successful. Then you carve out your territory, assemble your team, and do those things that result in reaching your goals. You don't wander around hoping or wishing for success, and you don't hire just anybody for your team.

For example, while expanding my multifamily and commercial real estate portfolio under the brand American Ventures (American-Ventures.com), I looked for a vice president of investments. I put word out—almost seven or eight months in advance—that I was looking for a top-notch candidate with both asset management and acquisitions experience in commercial real estate. I received résumés almost constantly over the next six months and ended up making a hire that I believe is excellent. All the résumés and the final candidate came from reaching out to my network.

Meeting Powerful Allies

In addition to joining organizations that focus on your interests and values, another great way to meet like-minded people is by attending conferences, fund-raising events, and speaking on panels; these aren't innovative suggestions, but they are worth emphasizing. Each type of event provides opportunities to meet allies in addition to members of your tribe. For example, being a member of TIGER 21 enables you to be part of events that high-profile people attend. These events range from afternoon talks, to three- to five-day leadership retreats, to events supporting a charitable cause. A big value from the retreats, in addition to the learning that goes on, is the long-term relationships that develop.

A VISIT TO NECKER ISLAND

One of my contacts was on the board of directors for Carbon War Room, which promotes low-carbon energy use to combat climate change. Carbon War Room, which Richard Branson and fellow entrepreneurs founded in 2009, is one of five NGOs that Virgin Unite helped create and continues to fund. A colleague in TIGER 21 is on the board of certain Virgin Unite events and worked with Richard Branson and other colleagues to develop a five-day leadership retreat on Necker Island. The event raised funds for Virgin Unite's initiatives, which it describes as "disruptive collaborations ... bringing together the right people to defy the status quo."[15] The fees for attending the retreat were split among The Elders, Carbon War Room, The B Team, Ocean Unite, and Unite BVI Foundation.

When you spend five days hanging out with like-minded people

---

15   Virgin Unite, "Virgin Unite and Tiger 21 Leadership Gathering," 2017.

on a private island, you tend to become friends. More than hanging out, though, we participated in training designed to inspire us to find purpose and take leadership roles to create a better world. During the workshops, we heard from a group of stellar speakers as well as the main host, Richard Branson. The topics were inspiring: "Answering the Call," "Purpose in Business," "Becoming a Movement Builder for Gender," "Purposeful Leadership," and "Purpose-Led Transformation." Early-morning sessions taught meditation and yoga. Some of the friendships that began on the retreat became enduring, and I still hang out with people from all over the country whom I met on the trip.

A highlight of the trip was talking with Richard Branson. He has inspired me for a long time, especially his thoughts about learning by doing and testing yourself by taking chances and pushing your boundaries. We connected through our diversified professional backgrounds, but the conversation revolved around many common interests.

Branson's investment in space travel is especially intriguing. I am fascinated by the new space industry and was deeply interested in speaking with Branson about Virgin Galactic. Not long before I talked with Branson about his space program, I viewed the SpaceX (Elon Musk's company) Falcon Heavy launch at Cape Canaveral, Florida; a few months prior with friends, I took a small plane tour of Jeff Bezos's Blue Origin site, close to Marfa, Texas. Branson and I talked about the competitive nature of the industry as it begins to develop and how collaboration might lead to faster progress in creating business models.

From the space industry, our discussions jumped to the future of life, advances in human genetics, and how our DNA reveals who our ancestors are.

I went to Necker Island to learn leadership skills that would enable me to incorporate purpose-driven action in my company and life. But social media opens your network and can produce unanticipated results. Photos of the event—some of me talking with Richard Branson—were on LinkedIn, Facebook, Instagram, and Twitter. Some real estate brokers saw the photos. When I flew back to Austin, I had a call with a broker selling a portfolio—sellers interview potential buyers to make sure they are selling a deal to the buyer who can close. On the call, the first thing the broker asked was, "How was your time with Richard Branson?" At the time of an interview with a seller, we have no idea how we are going to win that deal because we haven't secured the funds yet. But the association with Richard Branson subtly influenced the seller to think that in comparison to all other bidders, I had the team, the underwriting skills, and an ability to own and add value to properties that made me the best potential buyer.

MAKING CONNECTIONS AT CONFERENCES

Some of the organizations I associate with host invitation-only events—like the Necker Island retreat—and members pay substantial fees to attend, which in part support philanthropy. The speakers are committed to talking with the people attending; it is part of how they share what they've learned and give back to the business and philanthropic community.

The TIGER 21 annual meeting is packed with amazing speakers who make time to talk with people. Learning from wildly successful entrepreneurs is a significant benefit of the annual meetings and has influenced how I think about who to hire and how to find them. I met Mike Bloomberg at an annual meeting, where he was a guest speaker. We connected when he learned St. John's University is my alma mater; his son went to law school there.

Another benefit is having the opportunity to hang out with people who perform at the top of their fields. After David Rubenstein, the founder of Carlyle, interviewed Howard Schultz at our annual meeting, he was generous and hung out with us. The experience taught me that mentoring doesn't have to be a significant relationship that extends over months or years. It can happen in a simple conversation with a generous expert. At that time, we were thinking of selling a lot of our CRE assets, so I asked Rubenstein whether the decision to sell all our assets in the next twelve months was the right thing to do. He said, "Sell, sell, sell." The founder and chairman of a massive private equity real estate group has an amazing vantage point on the market. When he said "sell," it validated our decision. Even though it was a simple question to ask and a simple answer for him to give, it had a profound impact on my confidence that we were taking advantage of the peak of the market. Being in confidential surroundings rather than, say, an elevator, makes it possible for conversations like this to take place.

Sam Zell was a keynote speaker at another annual meeting. Following my usual bold approach—some people would call it brazen—I walked up to him and asked a question. He made time to hang out with some others and me for a half hour or so. We asked him different questions, and he told us that he had a book coming out. This was May 2017, and the book was *Am I Being Too Subtle?: Straight Talk from a Business Rebel.* Zell said, "I've done so many things in life but writing a book was one of the toughest." In fact, that conversation planted the seed for writing a book in my mind.

One of my TIGER 21 colleagues moderated a breakout session with Deepak Chopra at an annual meeting. He suggested that I attend the session and invited me to hang out with Chopra and him after the talk. Chopra is a successful Indian American, we both received our education in India, and he went on to achieve big things in life; I welcomed the chance to talk with him. Because the environment was relaxed and social, I was comfortable asking him questions. Early in my career, in addition to working as a research scientist in the pharmaceutical industry, I was involved in marketing pharmaceutical-grade nutritional supplements, sometimes referred to as nutraceuticals. So I asked Chopra what he thought about the role of supplements in maintaining and improving a person's health—as the saying goes, prevention is better than cure. I also mentioned that when I moved to the United States years ago, I saw his name and photograph on a book as I was walking through Barnes & Noble. Seeing his book inspired me to think about writing a book. After a few minutes of conversation, we ended up exchanging email addresses.

Later, when he was doing an event for the Chopra Foundation in Austin, I invited him to dinner. He couldn't make dinner since he was in Austin for only a few hours but said that he would love for me to attend the event he was hosting that evening and immediately connected me to the president of the Chopra Foundation. I was under the impression that this would be a small gathering, but when I arrived, I discovered it was a two thousand-person, sold-out event. Chopra did not have to go out of his way to arrange for me to attend a sold-out event. The experience taught me that a person of great stature can be greatly humble, a quality I often see in the most successful people.

In other circumstances, you meet skillful people at the top of their fields through business dealings. Francis Greenburger is a New York City real estate developer who invested in different parts of Manhattan, Queens, and Long Island City; he is also a literary agent, author, and philanthropist. His company, Time Equities, was looking to expand into the Texas market. We approached their firm to engage in potential joint-venture investments. At that time, we were putting together a contract for a deal. Although we were structuring the investment through intermediaries, after reading my profile, Greenburger invited me to meet with him. We spent forty-five minutes talking about what goes into making a good deal. It was a mentoring session with one of the great real estate investors. Everyone at the highest level in business looks at simple things, and Greenburger is no different. He asked what I was buying the deal for and what I would sell it for. He also wanted to know about the projected unlevered internal rate of return (IRR). However, it's quite common in the industry to look at levered IRR, ROI, and multiples of the return. I was looking more at buying and selling at capitalization rates that would give a yield of 200 or 250 basis points. He was asking me about a simple concept, and I didn't have the data to answer his question. The experience taught me a lot about being prepared for the unexpected. I made sure to send an email to him that afternoon after consulting with my analyst. Now that metric is part of our underwriting model.

One member of the Austin TIGER 21 group is on the board of the Andy Roddick Foundation (ARF). He and I are friendly and both enjoy tennis, so he invited me to his house to watch the Wimbledon and US Open tennis matches. I ended up sitting on the couch next to Andy Roddick, who was ranked first in world tennis singles in 2003 and won the US Open that year. When I learned about ARF's worthy causes, like providing educational support to youth living in East Austin, I was happy to support their unique 40-Love program. The program provides high-quality learning experiences that supplement school-based education for lower-income students. Educating the next generation—one of my father's principles—enables you to touch thousands of lives.

When I was growing up, one of our family pastimes was watching the Grand Slam tennis tournaments. The Wimbledon, Australian Open, French Open, and US Open tennis tournaments feature the best of the tennis world. When Andy hosted Roger Federer at a private and intimate get-together in Austin, I had a chance to spend time with Roger. As I am a big tennis fan, this was my grand slam, the best of the best.

Three themes weave through all these stories. First, when your goal is to assemble powerful allies to be the board of directors for your life, you must do things where powerful allies are also doing things, whether that is business, personal, or philanthropic. Second, you keep in touch with them through your shared interests. Third, your reputation precedes you. When you do high-quality work in your field, word gets around. When you give back to the community and share your wealth, whether it is knowledge or money, others join you.

WHEN YOU GIVE BACK TO THE COMMUNITY AND SHARE YOUR WEALTH, WHETHER IT IS KNOWLEDGE OR MONEY, OTHERS JOIN YOU.

These general points remain true regardless of your stage of life or career. You make acquaintances and friends by seeking out people who share your interests. Networking is a facet of this social activity with a more targeted focus, whether that is career or personal development. You attend events and join clubs that appeal to your interests and align with your goals. You make friends, and may even find a life partner, this way. Because everyone is in the same situation and started the same way, they are willing to help each other reach their goals and learn from each other.

You can take a thoughtful approach to networking. It involves choosing events to attend and preparing in advance. You might read a book or recent article by or about speakers who interest you. You might think of a few questions you might ask different speakers. You might be bold, send an email to a speaker, and suggest you meet.

The same thoughtfulness can have an impact when you are the invited speaker. Presenting or speaking as part of a panel exposes you to many people who might then want to network with you. You can take an organic approach to speaking engagements and participate when you are asked. Or you can be mindful about the time investment and choose only those engagements that will have the greatest positive impact.

This applies as well to sponsoring an event. Even though sponsoring takes a smaller time commitment, it still offers opportunities for networking. Being mindful about which events you sponsor can put you in a place where you will have a more impactful experience.

Giving Back

Basic education is free in most countries, including India. But in India the quality of the government-maintained schools is poor. Even as India became the fifth largest economy in the world, change happened slowly. When I was growing up, most families sent their children to private schools, which charge tuition. In the United States private school is a privilege, but in India the concept is different.

When my father was nearing retirement age, a couple approached him for help educating one of their children. The child scored in the top percentile—99.9 percent—to get a seat in medical school. With this highest merit level, tuition is subsidized so that the fee is minimal. But the parents could not afford to pay even minimal tuition. My father paid for the son's medical school, which is a four- to five-year program just like in the United States, up to the salaried internship.

About two years after the son entered medical school, his sister also scored in the 99.9 percentile on the entrance exam. It is amazing that two children from the same family put in the amount of hard work to achieve this distinction. The parents still did not have the financial means to pay the lowest medical school fee, so my dad paid for her schooling as well.

After completing medical school and specialty training with an outstanding record, the son had two options. He could work in a big corporate hospital in a big city and make lots of money from day one. Or he could go back to the small town where he grew up. Because there are not many medical facilities in that kind of area, it's a big opportunity, but it's riskier. So he went back and set up a practice in that town. He didn't take the easy path of working for a big hospital and making lots of money. Instead, he went back to that small-town community, which had less financial opportunity and greater risk. One part of his motivation for that choice, I'm sure, is giving back.

My father's experience was similar. He was the first medical doctor from his rural village. His grandparents and parents worked hard for their next generation. When I grew up near Hyderabad, our family was well off compared to most of the middle class in India; my father grew up in a family focused on business. My father's whole village knew the power of education. And when you know the value of education, you give back. My father's medical education was his village's legacy. They used their collective power to lift my father up. When he became wealthy, he passed that to others. The children he helped will touch hundreds of lives through their medical training, just as he did. Through his choices, my father taught me to value education and give back to the community.

When I got into real estate as an entrepreneurial venture, I decided to focus my business on workforce housing. It was a good strategy because the workforce always needs a place to live, regardless of what is happening elsewhere in the economy. When I moved from residential real estate to commercial real estate, I took that strategy with me. Over time, I developed a second strategy of following a city's path of gentrification.

Direct lessons from these gentrification-path deals prompted me to get involved in philanthropy in a big way. I learned a lot about the history of East Austin from exploring a deal there (which I described as a lesson in politics in chapter 5). Historically, Interstate Highway 35 divided Austin. Prime real estate with amazing buildings is on the west side of Interstate 35. Twenty years ago, when Austin was still a small town, the east side of the interstate was left out and became a low-income demographic area. For years, East Austin has been more like New Orleans. There are fantastic living spaces in one block, but the next block is left out. When development leaves out an area, it has a ripple effect. For example, the schools suffer. I wanted to find a way I could have a positive impact.

And then I met Andy Roddick and his foundation. Andy's educational foundation benefits children in the Austin school system by providing enriched activities after school, during spring break, and during summer when schools are closed. The foundation focuses on helping children find what they are good at, and programs span literacy, STEM, the arts, and sports. Andy invited me to the annual fund-raising gala, and I made a good-sized contribution through my businesses as well as a personal contribution. The foundation raised $1.6 million in 2017.

When I worked on residential real estate deals in San Antonio, I followed a strategy of doing good for many people while making a profit. My way of giving back was directly tied to my business. But just like my goal of scaling up in real estate, I wanted to scale up in philanthropy.

I also wanted to be strategic about it. Following my father's lead by investing in education was a start. One principle I adhere to is aligning myself with powerful allies—whom you associate with influences how successful you are. So, to build a philanthropy strategy, I looked at the actions of businesspeople whom I admire.

Consider Bill Gates, who made billions of dollars running Microsoft as profitably as he could. He and his wife, Melinda, along with Warren Buffett and other prominent billionaires, pledged to give away most of their wealth through philanthropy. As of 2017, the Bill & Melinda Gates Foundation provided $46 billion in grants in the United States and 130 other countries since it started in 2006. I aspire to be like my father, but also to be like Bill and Melinda Gates, Warren Buffett, and other great philanthropists.

I had already identified educating the next generation and helping them create opportunities as the area I want to work in. I also knew economic inequality in the United States and the country I grew up in is significant and has a growing negative impact on education. India spends about US$385 per student on primary and secondary education. The United States spends a little over $12,000 per student on primary and secondary education. In addition, girls in India—and other parts of the world—don't have the educational opportunities that they have in the United States. My philanthropy could have great impact in India.

When I looked around for a good organization to work through, I found Pratham USA. Pratham is organized by chapters in major cities, and I am a member of the Austin chapter's board.

"IF YOU EDUCATE A BOY, YOU LIFT HIS ENTIRE FAMILY. WHEN YOU EDUCATE A GIRL, YOU LIFT THEIR ENTIRE GENERATION."

Pratham—the word *first* in Sanskrit—has educational programs in twenty-one of India's twenty-nine states. Their programs focus on learning and literacy, girls' education, and vocational training. In India, like in a lot of other countries, educating girls becomes a second priority when there is another option. To overcome that bias, Pratham created centers in nine of India's states that focus on educating girls. There is a saying that summarizes how important this issue is: "If you educate a boy, you lift his entire family. When you educate a girl, you lift their entire generation." The idea behind this saying is that when women are educated, they make sure all their kids become educated. I also think there should be more women entrepreneurs in the world, which will help avoid and resolve some of the crises we face. Education is a strong basis for entrepreneurship.

The Pratham program, and similar programs, has benefits that ripple outward. When kids who get help grow up, they go out of their way to help others. The benefits inherently go way beyond the kids in the program because they pass it on. Their gratitude prompts them to think beyond themselves. They will spend their time and resources to help ten or more other people. It has a multiplying effect.

We live in a global economy. I received my education in India, but all the jobs I created are in the United States. I feel a natural gratitude for the powerful gift of education I received growing up. Educating underprivileged kids in India is the least I can do to repay. As the distances and divisions in the world economy are shrinking, I want to employ tactics I learned in the United States to create jobs in India.

Giving back isn't limited to donations to places you live in or grew up in; it isn't limited to sitting on the boards of big foundations. It also involves giving back to the community and places of worship you believe in. I donate to the local Hindu temple. I am a practicing Hindu, the religion that created Yoga and Ayurvedic medicine.

The intent is to support what you believe in. For example, I believe that everyone needs a place of worship, so I found a way to donate to a church in my area. I use the land near the Formula 1 racetrack for public parking during races. At first, I hired a parking lot management firm to run the lot, but it is a for-profit business. Then a nearby church proposed that they could manage the parking lot. In exchange for them doing all the work, we split the money we earn on parking.

My mother and father set an example of giving back to the community. I follow in their footsteps, whether that is locally or through philanthropic organizations that have global impact. My father directly benefited an entire village through his actions. He touched, and through me will touch, an entire generation and the generations that follow. He didn't give back with that in mind, and neither do I. We do it because it makes life meaningful.

EXECUTIVE SUMMARY

- Use a diligent and systematic approach to building an inner circle of friends and associates who will support all aspects of your life.

- Let your values guide whom you hang out with.

- Use a balanced approach to focus on the three pillars of life: personal development, professional development, and philanthropy.

- When networking, understand that you are connecting with other human beings; avoid taking a transactional approach to your relationships.

- Allow yourself to be vulnerable to develop deep connections with others. Taking chances and pushing your boundaries help develop your capacity for vulnerability.

- Frequently ask, "What am I doing with my life?" Listen to your and your friends' answers.

- To have good friends and a good mentor, be a good friend and a good mentee.

- Let your personal and professional interests guide the workshops, conferences, and events you attend. You'll find people who will become lifelong friends and allies.

- Remember that amazing, successful, or prominent people are human beings too. Let them know what you admire and value about them by asking them good questions.

- Give back to your community and help others around you. Philanthropy consists of contributing to organizations and personal, local action.

CHAPTER 8

UP AND OUT: STRETCHING LIMITS

T echnology and globalization have driven change in the United States over the past fifty years. One significant change has been the economic shift from the manufacturing sector to the service sector. Since the turn of the century, technology has increasingly disrupted industries across the economic spectrum. The financial industry has seen enormous change. The first ATM was deployed in Australia in 1969, and they became ubiquitous by the 1980s. Algorithmic trading hit the stock market with SEC approval in 1998. But the mid-2000s brought subprime mortgages, driven by low-interest rates and easy money, and derivative financial instruments, fueled by faulty risk models, which triggered a financial meltdown in 2007. Throughout this change and disruption, the real estate industry has weathered bubbles and slumps. People always need places to live and work, as I've said many times. With systematic observation and a good grasp of KPIs and OKRs, multifamily and commercial real estate remains a good investment. And with a lot of entrepreneurial hustle, you can create and scale great ventures.

Technology in Real Estate

BIG DATA

Technology is making the commercial real estate industry ever more efficient through its impact on data collection and sharing. For example, CoStar, a commercial real estate information company, leverages technology, research, and data analytics to provide competitive market information that helps dealmakers like American Ventures develop sound underwriting models. LoopNet and Zillow use mobile technology to get information on nearby available rentals to potential tenants and on commercial real estate deals to potential investors. A multitude of apps using mobile technology or simple but profound platforms like Craigslist reduce the amount of time it takes to match sellers with buyers and lessors with tenants. We all are aware of the disruption Airbnb or HomeAway, an Austin start-up, brought to the vacation or short-term rental industry. With technology, more good deals happen more quickly.

CROWDFUNDING

Whereas data collection and sharing technology improves the efficiency of the entire real estate industry, crowdfunding technology has a direct impact on real estate investing. By now, most people know what crowdfunding is. You use an internet platform to raise money from many people—the sums can be small—to fund your business or other venture, like art, music, or philanthropy. Crowdfunding hit the real estate investment industry in 2012 after Congress enacted the

Jumpstart Our Business Startups (JOBS) Act and the Security and Exchange Commission (SEC) approved the platform and loosened rules about advertising investment opportunities.

There are different types of investors, and the investment opportunities are broad. Accredited investors have the most reach. The SEC sets the rules for who is accredited, which aim to identify people who have enough financial knowledge to choose unregulated investments wisely; the criteria are two years of income exceeding $200,000 or net worth higher than $1,000,000 outside of a personal residence. The idea is for the investor to be able to bear the economic risk they are taking.

Prior to crowdfunding, investors got involved in financing commercial real estate in two ways. One was through real estate investment trusts (REITs), which are traded on financial markets. The other was finding a project to invest in via networking or word of mouth—a closed circle situation of syndicated deals through friends and family or country club deals with substantial minimum investments to participate in a deal. I explained how this works in chapter 2. In both cases, the investment opportunities involve multimillion-dollar projects.

Crowdfunding enables investments in smaller projects, like fix-and-flip businesses, and smaller apartment or commercial real estate buildings. It also enables investors to invest smaller amounts of money. For example, in the past I had the option to go with a small group of investors who put, say, $3,500,000 into my deal. With crowdfunding, a maximum of ninety-nine investors can participate in a deal, putting in as little as $5,000 to $10,000. The complexity involved in putting together a deal with ninety-nine investors makes it costly; the legal fees alone would be staggering.

This is where the crowdfunding platforms have come in. They raise funds efficiently and remove the complexity of putting together a deal with many small investors. Several big companies—for example,

Fundrise, Realty Mogul, and CrowdStreet—have developed platforms. Because the SEC rules are looser, these platforms can advertise to individual investors. They raise capital through their platform and deploy that capital through us or other operators in one chunk.

We raised over $20 million through crowdfunding platforms in 2016 and 2017. Putting together a crowdfunding deal is efficient. For example, to raise $2.5 million through syndicating a deal (see chapter 2), I would need to talk with one hundred different investors who put in $25,000 each. To raise the funds through crowdfunding, I talk only to one group like CrowdStreet, RealtyMogul, or Fundrise, and so on. These platforms raise the capital from accredited investors, who can provide larger sums of money, or there are groups that can accept funds from nonaccredited investors, who might provide as little as $500. The platform acts like a big institutional firm, which we usually raise funds from, but the money comes from many individuals.

Scaling Up to One Billion Dollars

At the peak of our dealings, we owned close to $300,000,000 of real estate. Recall that in our business model, we typically get 65 to 70 percent of the funding for any deal from lenders. Then we raise the remaining funds through institutional equity firms, high-net-worth individuals, family offices, and our own funds.

Using the same model, American Ventures's goal is to own one billion dollars' worth of real estate. How do we do that? Exactly like we have been doing over the past few years but more efficiently and faster. Because my team and I have been there and done it, we have a good track record. So now we can engage in more and bigger deals. Our track record enables this scaling—track record and reputation are everything.

In addition to track record, the economics of the real estate cycle make a difference. We are not in the same real estate cycle as five to seven or even twenty years ago. In the early 2000s, prior to the financial crisis in 2007–2008, institutions and investors made the highly flawed assumption that real estate values would only increase. No one considered what would happen if values decreased. Since banks were lending at very high loan-to-value ratios and the market assumed an unending increase in value, institutions threw underwriting standards out the window. People paid insane prices for properties because asset inflation would bail them out whether the investment was truly good or not. This is the nature of an asset bubble.

The whole real estate cycle was the equivalent of playing with house money. People took unnecessary and irresponsible risks because they got so much money from banks and had to put very little of their own money in the deal. If you put in very little money, what risk are you really taking?

Today, banks are more cautious about lending. Leverage ratios have decreased so that today you get a loan at 75 percent of asset value rather than 95 percent. In addition, banks carefully scrutinize underwriting, which makes it more involved. We need to be mindful of how these differences affect our deals.

Another fact that fuels diversification and scaling is access to bigger institutional equity. Formerly, we engaged with equity companies that invest, say, $2.5 to $5 million at a time. We brought in individuals who invest $100,000 to $250,000 at a time. Now, we need to magnify that scale. For example, we might engage with a company that invests a minimum of $20 million at a time. If an equity firm puts in $20 million and our company puts in, let's say, $1 million, then we get the remaining 65 to 70 percent from lenders. So that $20 million investment can give you access to almost $60 million or $70 million of assets. Bigger institutional equity fuels scaling in commercial real estate.

This financial scaling implies that American Ventures will be investing in and developing larger properties. We will also have the flexibility to increase the quality of the assets. For example, in the past we consistently acquired 200- to 250-unit deals. As we scaled, we acquired a 1,500-unit deal that consists of eight apartment complexes in different parts of Dallas–Fort Worth; these complexes were scattered to the northeast, southeast, middle, and south side of the metro area. During that acquisition, we acquired eight of those properties with several equity partners, each investing in one or two deals. As we scale, American Ventures will be open to acquiring a portfolio of 2,000 units, like that deal, and striking a strategic relationship with bigger equity partners that can create a joint venture with us on the entire portfolio. Hypothetically, acquiring five 2,000-unit portfolios gives you the critical mass to reach $1 billion.

Following the system in *Measure What Matters* is an important part of how I plan to scale American Ventures. John Doerr points out that objectives and key results (OKRs) yield better business results than simple goals and explains why this is the case. To turn the goal of $1 billion into an objective, all we need to do is add a time frame; to complete the OKR, we need to add milestones that specify how we'll achieve the objective. American Ventures' current OKR statement is:

Objective: Establish American Ventures LLC as a premier multifamily and commercial real estate investment company owning and operating a portfolio of assets in the select major and top-performing markets in the United States, as measured by:

KEY RESULTS

1. Create a portfolio of $1 billion of assets under ownership by fourth quarter 2021.

2. Partner with two institutional equity groups that can deploy upward of $25 million per investment.

3. Consistently deliver 20 percent IRR to our investors on typical three- to five-year hold periods.

When we closed the 1,500-unit deal, the funds came from private equity groups, family offices, and individual investors, and each of the eight properties had its own LLC as the buyer. As we expand, American Ventures will work with one investment group to buy all eight properties. In the first example, it took six to eight months to close each property because each property had a different investor. American Ventures's time frame to close in the future will be shorter.

We fund larger deals with bigger institutional equity groups, private equity groups, and funds that can write much bigger checks. They deploy their capital through us, and we become their local boots on the ground, managing the assets and portfolio. They could, and do, buy their own assets, or they might manage deals working through firms like us. To reach our goals, we achieve greater efficiency when we have one or two investor groups buying all the properties with us.

The operational process on our side is the same as described in chapter 2. All the work to put together a deal usually takes sixty to seventy-five days. During that time, we secure the best loan from a commercial lender, conduct the due diligence process (which takes thirty to forty-five days), and work out how to raise the money remaining after the loan. If we need to raise, say, $3 to $5 million after securing the loan, American Ventures would put in 5 to 10 percent of the equity capital and raise the remainder from private equity groups.

The private equity groups review the deal. They rely on us to provide all the initial information and feedback on the deal. Four groups, for example, might have an interest in the deal and ask for more details. At that point, we share all the pertinent details, including the underwriting models, photographs, business plan, and other supporting documentation, in an offering memorandum. They put our information into their models and then work together to decide what to pursue.

Just as we have a pipeline of deals, private equity groups might evaluate our deal along with ten others from different firms and reject five of them. Some reasons they reject a deal are timing, return profile, target area, age of the property, and so on. Sometimes they respond that a deal isn't for them without giving a reason.

The attractiveness of a deal is somewhat subjective. A deal that is unattractive to one group might be attractive to another. To overcome this issue, we establish or maintain relationships with an equity group and ask them directly what they want. We get detailed about the questions: What kind of returns or return profile are you looking for? What kind of assets do you look for? What is your typical hold time? What market do you want to play in? Some partners are interested in acquiring a portfolio of deals; some are interested in acquiring only individual deals. We maintain a list of each equity partner's criteria. Then when a deal comes along, we know whether it is a match and engage with that partner.

If they like the deal, they dig deeper. They have phone calls with us, and their analyst talks with our analyst to review the underwriting. If they like what they hear, they visit the property. If everything looks good at that point, they'll finally say, "Yes, let's make it happen." They might send a term sheet, and we'll develop an operating agreement together. Typically, we get the loan and act as the managing member or general partner. They act as a member or a limited partner.

Outlier situations are rare by definition but can occur. We might discover that what looked like a good deal turns out to be not so good after all. Maybe the property has structural flaws, or we may find issues not outlined in a property condition analysis or third-party reports. If the information we gather makes us think it's not a good deal after all, we tell both the lender and the equity partner. Usually, the equity partner is in touch with us throughout the due diligence process. They are fully informed, and we decide together if we should or should not pursue the deal. If we decide not to pursue the deal, we terminate the contract and get our earnest money back. In most of the primary markets in Texas, like Dallas–Fort Worth, Austin, Houston, and San Antonio, we may put down part of our earnest money deposit (EMD) as nonrefundable at the time of signing our purchase and sale agreement (PSA). Let us say on a $20 million deal, EMD is $250,000. $25,000 of that is nonrefundable after execution of the PSA, and of that $250,000, which we paid at signing, we get only $225,000 back. Even though nonrefundable EMD is not common in all markets, it has become common in high-growth markets over the last few years. From a seller's point of view, it indicates the seriousness of the buyer to acquire the property and provides more surety of closing. For the buyer, it's one way to win a deal in a highly competitive market and a way to differentiate from the rest of the buyer pool.

When a deal turns out to be unworkable, we may get most or all of our deposit back, terminate, and move on to the next deal. We engage in the due diligence process to identify the deals with problems and get out of them quickly. Equity partners appreciate that. The goal is to develop and implement the business plan, but if the due diligence process produces troubling results, it's wise to terminate and move on. No deal is better than a bad deal.

We build long-term relationships by operating in this transparent way, because it's obvious we're not in the deal to earn fees. We are in the deal to make profits for everyone.

WE ARE IN THE DEAL TO MAKE PROFITS FOR EVERYONE.

The process, down to the smallest detail, is the same whether you are doing a deal with two hundred units or two thousand units. We put in a lot of legwork and interact with a lot of lenders, private equity groups, real estate brokers, service providers, and our contractor groups while we put together a deal. Previously, we were growing through $10 to $15 million deals. Now our goal is to partner with companies that are looking for much bigger deals, like $25 to $30 million.

Global Markets in Commercial Real Estate

To scale up to one billion dollars, we need to take advantage of funding available from global markets. US commercial real estate—and in Texas—is extremely active, and the economy has grown more than expected, so our commercial real estate market is stronger than in other developed economies. By virtue of that, US commercial real estate is a prime destination for capital to flow in from other parts of the world—say, China, Canada, parts of Europe, or the Middle East, spearheaded by commercial hubs like London, Hong Kong, Singapore, or Dubai in the UAE. Right now, the United States is a very good place to reinvest capital. Just as we go to private equity groups to fund big projects, we want to target investors from China, Canada, UK, Japan, Germany, Dubai, and so on.

American Ventures, although a young firm compared to the likes of Blackstone or Carlyle, has already entertained a group of smaller

Chinese investors. We took them to one or two properties. Now we have trips planned to London, Hong Kong, Singapore, Dubai, and similar places, where we will connect with investors and have that avenue of capital available.

Expanding into Strategic Markets

Doing the same thing bigger will take us only so far. Working on deals only in Texas is limiting. Hindsight is twenty-twenty and gives us a good perspective. We entered the Texas multifamily market when it was right in the striking zone of the market cycle. By the time we grew the firm from nothing to four thousand units in the multifamily space, competitors had driven up the value of potential deals in these markets.

Exploring markets beyond the Austin–Dallas–Fort Worth–Houston–San Antonio metro areas is a strategic move. We are doing research to identify a location comparable to what Austin and Dallas were five years ago. For example, one of our investor groups identified twelve markets that are in a more advantageous part of the cycle. Going after those and similar markets will enable expansion. These institutional groups have access to more resources like market data, internal memos from their existing portfolio of assets, and key personnel to do market-specific studies at very micro- and macrolevels of each region. We align ourselves with groups like these to help us determine what specific markets to focus on.

Earlier, I discussed cases that showed how critical it is to have detailed information about the target investment area. You need to understand any political situations and the planned and actual paths of gentrification. Every city—and every submarket within a city—has property management companies. We depend on expert property management companies, which you hire for a fee, for day-to-day operations and localized information. We also do a lot of research on the target market and submarket.

Our experience in Texas taught us how much high-quality information and talent we need. Texas is the second biggest real estate market in the United States; think of Texas as a country by itself. Consider that we own properties in quite a few primary, secondary, and tertiary markets in Texas, including Dallas–Fort Worth, Austin, San Antonio, Houston, Corpus Christi, and the Killeen–Waco area. The operational model we use here scales. To extend our market coverage, we will add to our core team an extremely experienced and talented local analysis and management team who will cover several specific markets. They will do the same thing we do in Texas: look at the property with us, visit the comparables, and, once a deal is closed, visit the property at regular intervals. The fundamentals of the Texas market apply to all markets.

Let's say I'm investing in Nashville, Tennessee, looking at three or four properties. When we begin the process, we will hire somebody local. Initially, our team from Austin and Dallas will visit back and forth. Success in this new market calls for having a good property management company but also depends on a good asset manager well versed in that market. Potential weaknesses in implementing this model are not having enough local people on staff or not having enough local knowledge. We overcome these weaknesses by doing a lot of high-quality research and hiring local talent. It goes back to the principle of working to your strengths and hiring for your weaknesses.

Following Demographic Trends to Diversify

Using technology to improve efficiency, scaling up, and entering strategic markets take business expansion only so far. Multifamily commercial real estate—apartment complexes—are a conventional investment. So are office buildings—I have limited office building investments in downtown Austin—and land investments. I focused on these conventional investments because of the access to capital. There was good historical information about the real estate cycle, so we were able to buy deals at a good value.

How can I diversify further? One answer is to explore other parts of multifamily housing, particularly senior housing. Senior housing looks like a good bet because more and more people in the baby boom generation are retiring.

RETIRING BABY BOOMERS

Baby boomers' housing needs and plans are diverse. Some are retiring and want to downsize, but at older ages than in earlier decades.[16] Younger baby boomers have no immediate plans to downsize—possibly 43 to 52 percent of them—or retire in the near future—around 20 percent.[17] When baby boomers finally retire in their eighties, continuing to live in a big house where they are responsible for maintaining the plumbing, heating, yard, and so on may not even be feasible.

---

16   Jessica Guerin, "Baby Boomers Won't Downsize Homes Anytime Soon," *Housingwire*, September 6, 2018, https://www.housingwire.com/articles/46757-baby-boomers-wont-downsize-homes-anytime-soon.

17   Paul Davidson, "More Baby Boomers Stay in Their Homes as They Reach Retirement, Skipping Downsizing," *USA Today*, May 21, 2019, https://www.usatoday.com/story/money/2019/05/21/home-buying-many-boomers-choose-age-place-and-not-move/3698390002/.

Other demographic information suggests that their children, many of them in the millennial generation, live closer to big urban centers.[18] Living an hour away in the suburbs makes life challenging for older parents—for example, transportation to needed services is in short supply—and their adult children. Baby boomers' diverse needs and plans create opportunities for new multifamily housing scenarios.[19] Traditional senior housing can provide necessary caretaking if adult children live far away, if the seniors have no children, or they are not able to live independently. Baby boomers as a generation hold the most wealth in the economy[20] and are driving changes in multifamily and senior housing everywhere.

There are different varieties of housing for senior living. One of them is called Active Adult or 55+, which is just like an apartment complex, but legally age restricted. Another is a continuing care retirement community, which offers a continuum from independent living cottages and apartments to assisted living and nursing care. There are also memory care facilities that provide different levels of services for seniors with dementia or Alzheimer's.

The investment model for these different types of senior housing is the same as for traditional apartment complexes, but senior housing is more operationally intensive. The same loans from Fannie Mae and Freddie Mac are available. The big difference is that operating costs are higher, so the way you manage the asset is different. Net operating

---

18 Paul Katzeff, "Here Are the Most Popular Neighborhoods Among Millennials," *Investor's Business Daily*, September 28, 2018, https://www.investors.com/etfs-and-funds/personal-finance/where-do-millennials-live-where-are-millennials-moving-to/.

19 Deborah Kearns, "Baby Boomers Are Struggling to Downsize and It Could Create the Next Housing Crisis," *Bankrate*, September 10, 2018, https://www.bankrate.com/mortgages/baby-boomer-downsizing-housing-crisis/.

20 Raymond Fazzi, "Baby Boomers Control Most of US Wealth, Report Says," *Financial Advisor*, March 28, 2019, https://www.fa-mag.com/news/baby-boomers-control-majority-of-u-s--wealth--report-says-44070.html.

income works the same way, but the expenses are higher from the start. For example, if expenses on a conventional apartment complex are 45 to 55 percent of gross revenue, they may be higher than that in senior housing. However, if you're looking at higher expenses, all you need to create a good deal is increase the revenue enough to have higher NOI. That is, if you can get the same returns as with investing in conventional apartment complexes, senior housing makes a good investment.

THE MILLENNIAL GENERATION

Another demographic trend influencing the housing market and general economy is the housing choices of the millennial generation. Some reports say that homeownership is out of reach for the millennial generation. A 2018 report from the Urban Institute points out that homeownership among millennials is 8 to 9 percent lower than in previous generations and for complex reasons.[21] One of them is that

REGARDLESS OF THE REASONS, THE GREATEST PERCENTAGE OF RENTERS COMES FROM THE MILLENNIAL GENERATION.

millennials tend to live in urban centers where homeownership costs are high and fewer homes are available to buy. Because millennials tend to live in urban centers, rents are also higher, which means more of their income goes to housing. They also carry a high student loan burden. These factors make it more difficult to save enough money to make a down payment on a home. Regardless of the reasons, the greatest percentage of renters comes from the millennial generation.[22]

---

21 Jung Hyun Choi, Jun Zhu, Laurie Goodman, Bhargavi Ganesh, and Sarah Strochak, "Millennial Homeownership: Why Is It So Low, and How Can We Increase It?" *Urban Institute*, July 2018, https://www.urban.org/research/publication/millennial-homeownership.

22 Alan Ehrenhalt, "City or Suburbs? What Do Millennials Really Want?" *Governing*,

What appears to be a downside for the residential housing market might be an upside for the rental market. I have good reason to think that people in their twenties to late thirties are more interested in flexibility than in homeownership. That's one implication of the preference for living in urban centers.

Millennial demographic trends are driving innovation in multi-family housing. One recent development is microunit housing, which includes a kitchen, bedroom, and bathroom in three hundred to three hundred fifty square feet. Buildings designed for microunit housing are going up in big urban centers like New York, Boston, Austin, and Seattle. A related innovation combines microhousing with coliving, in which residents share kitchen and living space amenities and services like house cleaning and communal events are available. Many developers are building these multifamily residences using prefabricated technology.

Another innovation is a completely mixed-use building, what's called "live, work, flex." These buildings have living space in one area and working space in another area, say downstairs from the apartments. This arrangement provides great flexibility, including short-term rentals. People are willing to pay a premium to live in small places with luxury amenities, communal space, and access to all the cultural benefits of an urban center. Some buildings have "apartment-crawl" events once a month, in which residents open their apartments to entertain other residents, which promotes making new friends. A

April 2018, https://www.governing.com/columns/assessments/gov-millennials-cities-suburbs.html.

Kriston Kapps, "Do Millennials Prefer Cities or Suburbs? Maybe Both," *CityLab*, July 2018, https://www.citylab.com/equity/2018/07/will-millennials-stay-downtown/566078/.

Richard Fry, "5 Facts about Millennial Households," *FactTank* (blog), Pew Research Center, September 6, 2017, https://www.pewresearch.org/fact-tank/2017/09/06/5-facts-about-millennial-households/.

sense of community is both driving and springing up around these mixed-use environments.

We are currently exploring creating a high-density microunit development. Because the development is close to downtown Austin, you can have higher density of units and fewer parking requirements. If residents live only a mile from downtown, they can walk or use a good public transportation system, scooters, a bike-sharing system, ridesharing apps like UberPool or Lyft Line, or a car-to-go system that you rent per mile and leave in designated spots.

SINGLE-FAMILY HOME TRENDS

Even with increasing retirement in the baby boom generation and new housing trends in the millennial generation, homeownership is still a priority for many people. After all, that's ingrained in the American Dream. The homeownership rate in 2018 was a little over 64 percent. The average over the past fifty years was a little over 65 percent. This stable trend makes single-family housing another opportunity, especially if we can create economies of scale. For example, there is a market for portfolios of homes in the same neighborhood. Lenders are providing loans for portfolios of single-family homes that are like the loans they provide for apartment complexes.

However, there are problems to solve with a portfolio of single-family homes. For example, in the Austin market, single-family homes are trading high. Another issue is that a portfolio of homes can require too much management for lower returns. Not all portfolio acquisitions may provide a viable business plan. One option that might address some of these issues is a portfolio of, say, one hundred homes in a neighborhood that would be good for renters.

HUMAN LONGEVITY

Scientific advances that are developing today are likely to increase the healthy lifespan of an individual. I am very optimistic about breakthroughs in scientific innovations that are happening in the area of human longevity. Many people are already living well into their nineties, but they have many health challenges, hence a need for senior housing. Within ten to twenty years, longevity science will help people live vibrantly for much longer. I follow this area for two reasons. First, my interest in pharmaceutical and health sciences has never waned. Second, increased longevity is bound to have an impact on people's housing needs. If baby boomers increase their healthy lifespan, they are less likely to retire. Although that might solve some economic problems, the potential impact on real estate requires some thought.

Why do I believe we are so close to longevity that people in commercial real estate should monitor the trend? Breakthroughs in science and medicine that boost our understanding of aging are coming at an increasingly rapid pace. The 2015 Nobel Prize in Chemistry was awarded to three scientists who advanced our understanding of DNA repair.[23] The longevity research company Calico, supported with funding from Alphabet, Google's parent company, is combining information from human genome sequencing with research on the microbiome to draw a picture of what healthy aging looks like.[24] According to Peter Diamandis, founder and executive chairman of the XPRIZE Foundation, research advances tested in mice models and

---

23   Matt Kwong, "Five Major Advances the Next Ten Years Will Bring," *Intel* (blog), *Reuters*, November 18, 2015, https://www.reuters.com/article/tr-pr-advances/five-major-advances-the-next-10-years-will-bring-idUSKCN0T72SK20151118.

24   Vivek Wadhwa, "Medicine Will Advance More in the Next 10 Years Than It Did in the Last 100," *SingularityHub*, October 26, 2016, https://singularityhub.com/2016/10/26/medicine-will-advance-more-in-the-next-10-years-than-it-did-in-the-last-100/#sm.0000ipymwlxxgdq4rsk2dyken8y9q.

human trials show we are very close to treatments that will cure cancer and chronic diseases like diabetes, sickle cell disease, and HIV. He also pointed out that research reported in *Nature*, experiments conducted at the Salk Institute, and therapies being developed at Alkahest provide strong evidence that we are on the verge of extending human life.[25] Usually, when scientific breakthroughs begin to converge, the chances that an advance will happen are high.

You might think that advances in longevity won't have much impact on housing because only wealthy people will benefit from longevity. But the pace of change is rapid. It may take a few years to develop an effective financing option—think of how financing the iPhone and other smartphones propelled their use—but once that happens, the price will come down. When the price comes down, mass adoption will occur, and the price will continue to fall.

There might also be different options for achieving longevity that are on offer at different price points. This model is like what you see in travel and cars. Some people travel all over the world at reasonable or even low cost—think of the book *How to Travel the World on $50 a Day*—and others take luxury trips. People buy different types of cars, from basic to ultraluxurious. The current mind-set in companies that are developing longevity technology is to make it available and affordable for everyone. Perhaps funding from governments or NGOs will step in to make it affordable, because longevity advances could produce a large social disparity.

Interestingly, an increasing problem in developed countries is that the birth rate is not keeping up with aging of the population—experts are calling this the "baby bust."[26] Some countries are experiencing a

---

25 Peter Diamandis, "Top Ten Tech Trends Transforming Humanity," *Tech Blog*, accessed June 7, 2019, https://www.diamandis.com/blog/top-10-tech-trends-transforming-humanity.

26 Peter Kotecki, "10 Countries at Risk of Becoming Demographic Time

shortage of younger people to sufficiently support economic growth. A lack of sufficient economic growth will reduce everyone's quality of life. But increased healthy longevity will enable people to be economically productive for many more years.

When longevity science begins to yield results over the next ten years, we will have some important questions to answer. For example, what impact will greater longevity have on people's housing needs? Will people who live into their hundreds develop distinct lifestyles like the millennial generation has? Today, seniors can't maintain single-family homes for health reasons, so they transition to senior housing. But long-lived seniors who are healthy won't need senior housing; they will need something different. Will they gravitate toward microunit communal living?

If people are longer-lived and healthy, they may want to work for many more years. This opens the door to another living option: the live-workplex. A live-workplex is an area designed for living and working, with everything you need within walking distance.

There are also master plan communities that have a combination of residences, workspaces, and business space, including a neighborhood medical center, all in one walkable location. One example is the Mueller Neighborhood in Austin, which is a growing "town-in-town" development at the Robert Mueller Municipal Airport site, an old decommissioned Austin airport. A master plan community has town homes, bigger homes with yards, apartment complexes, parks and other green space, coffee shops, restaurants, hotels, and a community area to hold performances, all coexisting in the heart of the city. One

Bombs," *Business Insider*, August 8, 2018, https://www.businessinsider.com/10-countries-at-risk-of-becoming-demographic-time-bombs-2018-8.

Caitlin Cheadle, "Fertility Rates Keep Dropping and It's Going to Hit the Economy Hard," *Visual Capitalist*, November 25, 2016, https://www.visualcapitalist.com/fertility-rates-dropping-economy/.

innovation might be zoning that enables fitness trainers to teach classes in parks, so fitness-oriented small businesses don't need to rent space in a building. A town-in-town development is a comprehensive living and working arrangement, but not in one concrete structure. Although the Mueller development is an urban community in a central-city location, similar living concepts are popping up in suburban areas, say, forty minutes outside of the core city.

At the heart of implementing these plans is a public-private partnership between city planning and commercial real estate development. A 2018 Brookings Institution report describes a trend of catalytic development that is producing revitalized urban areas that the authors, Christopher B. Leinberger and Tracy Hadden Loh, call "WalkUPs," short for walkable urban developments.[27] WalkUPs are being developed across the United States, including in Detroit, Michigan; Chattanooga, Tennessee; Cincinnati, Ohio; Seattle, Washington; Cambridge, Massachusetts; and Phoenix, Arizona.

TO CREATE A FUTURE THAT YOU WANT TO LIVE IN, YOU NEED TO THINK NOW ABOUT DIFFERENT IDEAS.

When we talk about twenty-five years in the future, we can only speculate. We can make good guesses that there will be space travel and people will live longer. But we can't know how housing will change and what impact that will have on the economy.

To create a future that you want to live in, you need to think now about different ideas.

---

27 Christopher B. Leinberger and Tracy Hadden Loh, *Catalytic Development: (Re) creating Walkable Urban Places* (The Brookings Institution, 2018). Christopher Leinberger is a land use analyst, and Tracy Hadden Loh is a data scientist. Both are on the faculty of the Center for Real Estate and Urban Analysis at the George Washington University School of Business.

REAL ESTATE IN SPACE

As a space nerd, I follow the space industry closely. As a kid, I learned the history of the US-USSR space rivalry and followed NASA. JFK's speeches on space exploration inspired me and left a lasting impact on my outlook. My conversations with Richard Branson when he hosted us at Necker Island revolved around space (Virgin Galactic). I read Elon Musk's biography twice and found his journey from immigrant to creator of innovative companies like Tesla and SpaceX incredible, almost superhuman by many standards. In 2018, a few Austin entrepreneurs and I chartered a plane to watch the Falcon Heavy launch; at the time, the Falcon Heavy was the biggest, most powerful rocket out there.[28] In a test of its payload capability, the Falcon Heavy that launched in February 2018 carried a Tesla Roadster and mannequin (named Starman) into orbit around the sun. According to Mike Wall, writing on Space.com, "The Roadster is journeying on an elliptical path, which takes it out beyond Mars at aphelion (the most distant point from the sun) and near Earth's orbit at perihelion (closest solar approach)."[29]

SpaceX has ambitious goals: traveling to Mars, establishing a base there, and eventually building a city and the infrastructure needed for it to thrive. I am inspired by what's coming up in the SpaceX and other space companies' pipelines, particularly the Big Falcon Rocket. One of my favorite quotes from Elon Musk is, "You want to wake up in the morning and think the future is going to be great—and that's what being a spacefaring civilization is all about. It's about believing

---

28 George Dvorsky, "Falcon Heavy Now Officially the Most Powerful Rocket in the World," *Gizmodo*, February 6, 2018, https://gizmodo.com/spacex-s-falcon-heavy-rocket-takes-off-1822770189.

29 Mike Wall, "A Year After SpaceX's 1st Falcon Heavy Launch, Starman (and a Tesla) Sail On," Space.com, February 6, 2019, https://www.space.com/43242-spacex-falcon-heavy-starman-tesla-launch-anniversary.html.

in the future and thinking that the future will be better than the past. And I can't think of anything more exciting than going out there and being among the stars."[30] These advances provide travel benefits within our planet as well. SpaceX has plans to shorten travel times between major cities on our planet to under an hour—for example, New York to Shanghai in thirty-nine minutes or Tokyo to New Delhi in thirty minutes. It's just a concept right now, but when that happens, it may create a completely new ecosystem of real estate investment.[31]

Some of the great scientists of the twentieth and twenty-first centuries, including physicist Gerard K. O'Neill,[32] astronomer Carl Sagan, theoretical physicist and cosmologist Stephen Hawking, physicist and futurist Michio Kaku, biochemist Robert Shapiro, and astrophysicist Neil deGrasse Tyson, have advocated for space colonization. Despite their advocacy over nearly fifty years, we haven't made much progress.

Although government programs fund research and development and NASA has taken us far, Branson, Musk, and Bezos think it will take more to launch humanity into space. They are building a new commercial industry and experimenting with different business models to help humankind realize the dream of establishing extraterrestrial outposts in the solar system and Milky Way galaxy. I agree with them. Establishing bases and building a city and infrastructure on another planet

---

30 Elon Musk, SpaceX.com, accessed May 28, 2019, https://www.spacex.com/mars.

31 SpaceX, "Starship | Earth to Earth," YouTube.com, September, 2017, https://www.youtube.com/watch?v=zqE-ultsWt0.

32 Veronique Greenwood, "The Men Who Made Space Colonies Look Like Home," *Discover*, February 27, 2013, http://discovermagazine.com/2013/jan-feb/0-space-colonies.

   Space Studies Institute, History, accessed March 28, 2019, http://ssi.org/about/history/.

   SSI 50: The Space Settlement Enterprise, accessed March 28, 2019, http://ssi.org/ssi-50-the-space-settlement-enterprise/.

or in space will take an army of skilled workers. That workforce will need somewhere to live, an innovative form of multifamily housing. Whether commercial multifamily housing ventures are innovative or off planet, it takes massive funding to create, sustain, and maintain them. And whether these ventures are on Earth or elsewhere, the DNA of multifamily and commercial real estate investing remains the same.

EXECUTIVE SUMMARY

- Stay informed about how technology is impacting your industry and experiment with new technologies.

- Closely follow cutting-edge changes in your industry so that disruption does not take you by surprise. If possible, experiment with potentially disruptive technology or processes.

- Spend time reading the predictions of futurists and discussing their ideas.

- Keep informed about trends in industry, economics, and society and consider the impact these trends may have on your industry.

- Look for opportunities for change and disruption.

ACKNOWLEDGMENTS

THANKS TO THE FOLLOWING PEOPLE:

Dr. Sudershan Parsi, Sujatha Parsi, Sri Latha Nerella, Radha Krishna Nerella, Sanjay Parsi, Vineetha Vasudevan, Swetha Erramshetty, Rahul Erramshetty, Vamsee Krishna Nerella, Dr. Lakshmi Sravani Nerella, Sejal Parsi, Vidul Parsi, Iha Erramshetty, Vivan Erramshetty, Megan Doherty, Ruby Parsi, Mushu Doherty, Mark Hansen, Jake Heffelfinger, George Jalil, Kerry Watson, Dale Jacobson, Glenn Gonzales, Heidi Gonzales, Vivy Nguyen, Mike Woodfield, John James, Leslie Morrison, Michael Izenberg, Jagdeep Grewal, Brian Sample, Rahul Patel, Grant Gaines, Drew Senulis, Danny Sanchez, Kenia Sanchez, Edward Springman, Jan Hansen, Bill Wagner, Tom Armstrong, David Osborn, Christopher Ryan, Richard Bennett, Michael Griffin, Michael L. Green, Steve Kuhn, Jeff Lamkin, Dustin McArthur, Bruce St John, Peter Strauss, Mike Rovner, Steve David, Mike Dillard, Chris Shonk, Adam Witty, Paige Cornetette, Depinder Grewal, Felix Ortiz, Ash Kumar, Jay Young, Joel Katz, John Foresi, Lisa Harris, Lisa Falzone, Sean Haynes, Maxwell Drewer, Peter Kirby, Pierce Nunley, Tatianna Jitkoff, Travis Hollman, Stephanie Hollman, Mike Garcia, Radhal

Krishna Alla, Jeff Devoll, Bob Ainslie, Dawn Ainslie, Mike Garcia, James McQuiston, Suman Singh, Jerry Dunlap, Ron Glaser, Russel Hinds, Blake Dunlap, Joshua Ross, Andrew Hartman, Marc Brutten, Travis King, Bom Emri, Darcy Gunnell, Cameron Lamming, Jonathan Chasson, Shannon Haines, Clark Cannon, Scott West, Elaine Shi, Roy Shi, Jason Hall, Annette Ham, Amy Fryer, Matt Norman, Ivan Kaufman, Jay Porterfield, Doug Gunn, Sanjay Chandra, Luke Moffitt, Alan Stalcup, John Arrow, Steve Adler, Diane Land, Andy Roddick, J. J. Langston, Ram Devineni, Kelly Witherspoon, Ashish Gupta, Vandana Kumar, Jovitha Franklin, Matt Andersen, Jeremy Mosier, Ramesh Kalwala, Raghu Kadasani, Madhusudhan Kopparapu, Shireesha Thangada, Brinda Tammara, Vijay Tammara, Ethin Ilan, Christopher S. Christian, Narsimha Telukuntla, Bujjibabu Godavarthi, Bhaskar Godavarthi, Natha Fort, Peter Avalos, Laura Avalos, John Lunceford, Brahmananda R. Thodati, Srinivas R. Thodati, Anup Raja Sarabu, Venkata Raja Panchumarthi, Vijay Thangada, Brian Esquivel, Adelina Rosen, Chuck Taylor, Bard Hoover, Ben Davis, Raymond Lord, Drew Kile, Al Silva, Taylor Snoddy, James Roberts, Mark Allen, Forrest Bass, Matt Phol, Richard Hall, Marvin Hegar, Stan Dziga, Debbie Dziga, Michael Dadashi, Ylianna Dadashi, Kyle Christian, Jackie Cartwright, Richard Wilson, Steve Glener, Richard Branson, Sam Zell, Michael Bloomberg, Frances Greenberger.

ABOUT
THE AUTHOR

Shravan Parsi is an entrepreneur and innovator with a background in the diverse fields of real estate investing and pharmaceutical research. His experience as a pharmaceutical scientist drives his systematic approach to multifamily and commercial real estate investing. Shravan has been involved in Texas real estate since 2003 and, as of 2019, has acquired several apartment complexes (with an aggregate of more than four thousand units) and several commercial properties by co-investing with private equity groups, family offices, high-net-worth individuals, and accredited investors.

Shravan is the CEO and founder of American Ventures (AmericanVentures.com). With a forecasted pipeline of $250 million in planned acquisitions for 2019/2020, American Ventures is positioned for aggressive growth. American Ventures offers private equity firms, family offices, and accredited investors access to quality multifamily and commercial real estate investment opportunities. Shravan's unique blend of scientific, management, and real estate experience informs American Ventures's strategic business vision. Shravan has founded and invested in several companies in single family real estate, multifamily and commercial real estate, biotech, and medical devices.

Born in India, Shravan developed a lifelong interest in business and investing from watching his father, a medical doctor, invest in real estate. Shravan holds a master's degree from St. John's University in New York and a bachelor's degree from Manipal Academy of Higher Education.

The Science of the Deal: The DNA of Multifamily and Commercial Real Estate Investing (scienceofthedeal.com), published by Forbes-Books, is Shravan's first book. Forbes is considered to be the market leader in business print and digital media. *Austin American-Statesman* featured Shravan as a value investor for his CRE investment adjacent to a Formula 1 racetrack prior to the inaugural US Grand Prix in Austin, Texas. He has been a featured speaker at *Texas CEO Magazine*'s Enlightened Speaker Series event. Shravan is a member of TIGER 21 and Central Texas Angel Network (CTAN) and is a past member of the Entrepreneurs' Organization (EO).

Educating underprivileged kids has become Shravan's greatest passion. He was inspired by his parents, Dr. Sudershan Parsi and Sujatha Parsi, who educated two kids who eventually became medical doctors. Shravan serves on the board of the Austin chapter of Pratham USA, whose mission is "every child in school and learning well," and he is also a member of 40-Love group of the Andy Roddick Foundation, with a vision of "a world where all young people have endless opportunities to realize and achieve their potential."

OUR
SERVICES

AMERICAN VENTURES LLC

American Ventures LLC is a multifamily and commercial real estate investment company focused on the acquisition, rehabilitation, and operation of value-add and core asset investment properties. American Ventures offers private equity firms, family offices, and accredited investors access to quality multifamily and CRE investment opportunities. With its commitment to its core values, American Ventures has earned local, regional, and national recognition in the multifamily and commercial real estate investment industry.

If you want to invest in multifamily and commercial real estate please visit **WWW.AMERICANVENTURES.COM** or please send us an email at **INVEST@AMERICANVENTURES.COM**.

THE SCIENCE OF THE DEAL: THE DNA OF MULTIFAMILY AND COMMERCIAL REAL ESTATE INVESTING

Stay up to date by visiting **WWW.SCIENCEOFTHEDEAL.COM** or send us an email at **INFO@SCIENCEOFTHEDEAL.COM**.

STAY IN TOUCH

SHRAVAN PARSI

LinkedIn: linkedin.com/in/shravanparsi/

Facebook: Shravan Parsi's page or facebook.com/realshravan/

Instagram: @realshravan

Twitter: @ShravanParsi

SCIENCE OF THE DEAL

Twitter: @scienceofdeal

Facebook: facebook.com/thescienceofthedeal